The Five Step Exit

The Skills You Need to Leave a Narcissist, Psychopath, or Other Toxic Partner and Recover Your Happiness Now

Amber Ault, Ph.D., MSW

Only she who does not choose is the loser in the end.

--- Adrienne Rich

ISBN-13:
978-0982605332

ISBN-10:
0982605331

AMBER AULT

:

"Sorrow prepares you for joy. It violently sweeps everything out of your house, so that new joy can find space to enter. It shakes the yellow leaves from the bough of your heart, so that fresh, green leaves can grow in their place. It pulls up the rotten roots, so that new roots hidden beneath have room to grow. Whatever sorrow shakes from your heart, far better things will take their place."
-Rumi
,

CONTENTS

INTRODUCTION

For most of us, ending relationships isn't easy. Ironically, if your relationship is especially toxic, getting out and moving on feels even harder. If your friends and family know what's happening, they have wondered for quite some time why you stay in a situation that involves so much unnecessary pain, drama, and exploitation. Whether you share your relationship troubles or keep your confusion and suffering to yourself — perhaps to protect your partner's reputation, perhaps from your own embarrassment — you probably ask yourself the same question: if things hurt so much all the time, why can't I just leave? Why can't I jump off of this rollercoaster?

Toxic relationships differ from relationships that simply involve a challenging match. They differ from partnerships in which people grow apart. Toxic relationships involve unhealthy imbalances of power and control, manipulation, deception, exploitation, drama, and other behaviors most of us would consider abusive. In ordinary relationships, endings involve sadness, anger, and grief. In toxic relationships, endings often involve fear, protracted problems, and ongoing emotional challenges for partners like you.

What makes it so difficult to leave a toxic relationship?

A pattern of inconsistent behavior psychologists call "intermittent reinforcement" makes leaving toxic relationships very difficult. Sometimes your partner's behavior feels unkind, unpleasant, volatile, and abusive. At other times you find relief or delight in your partner's charm, care, or sexual attention. If your partner were awful all the time, you would have left long ago. When your partner behaves like your dream mate, they give you hope that their lying, cheating, financial exploitation, yelling, and verbal or physical abuse

1

represent some kind of bizarre anomaly that can be explained as an extreme response to stress or a crazy childhood or a medical issue — or all of these at once. But as the unpleasantness becomes more chronic and the kindness becomes more rare, you start to suspect that your beloved gives no priority on treating you well. Instead, they show interest or concern or affection only when it's necessary to keep you hanging on. Intermittent reinforcement keeps us hopeful and in denial, like the dog whose abusive human occasionally tosses out a treat to keep the pup ever hopeful that a happy life with kind rewards will grow from unjustified loyalty.

Fear also keeps people from exiting toxic relationships. Sometimes people fear that their toxic partner will harm or torment them or their children or animals. Other times, they fear that the toxic partner will "go off the deep end" and hurt or kill themselves. They believe they would be responsible if this happened. If the possibility of ending your relationship raises these fears for you, these anxieties themselves confirm the toxic nature of your relationship. Nonetheless, you must address these fears as you make your exit plan, so you can respond skillfully to any threatening or risky situation that arises.

Finally, people often feel great resistance to leaving, even when they know things are horrible, because they have lost touch with their ability to imagine how things will improve following a break-up. This is understandable: circumstances are difficult now, and the journey ahead looks arduous. Much remains unknown about how difficult things will become if you exit. In the midst of the current situation, and anticipating a difficult parting, you may forget who you were before this relationship or find it difficult to envision how much better your life can be when you are free.

As a psychotherapist, I work with people in toxic relationship circumstances that threaten their very health and safety. While exiting seems the logical, life-saving choice to outsiders, living in the relationship over the course of time can erode your willpower, optimism, and confidence so that even leaving to save your health or life does not always appear an obvious choice to you as the person living inside a relationship nightmare.

Leaving may mean a change in your material quality of life; it may affect your job or your mortgage or your credit score — at least temporarily. Sometimes these measurable concerns become the focus for people mired in toxic relationships. Because of the abuse and constriction toxic relationships create for victims, these external measures of success and stability feel very important to preserve. However, nobody should have to make the choice between their health, sanity, or retirement fund and their relationship. If you currently face these alternatives, I hope you will choose your own welfare over persisting in a relationship that is destroying you. The sooner you get free, the more quickly you will recover.

I designed *The Five Step Exit* to help you evaluate your options for leaving a toxic relationship. You may be leaving because your partner's behaviors meet the clinical criteria for narcissistic, anti-social, or borderline personality disorder, whether or not they have formally been diagnosed. You may not think that your partner has a personality disorder, but nonetheless recognize that your toxic relationship can't be substantially transformed, and that you are unable to make yourself happy in it as it exists.

This book will help you prepare to leave while protecting yourself as much as possible and minimizing further damage to you and the other people in the situation. The book is divided into several sections; each section includes specific practices that will help you prepare to reclaim your life by exiting a toxic relationship and to recover afterwards. You may need some sections more than others, depending on where you are in the process, so feel free to start with the sections you most need now.

This book doesn't spend much time exploring what makes partners cruel and self-centered, unable to attach to or empathize with others, or comfortable exploiting and harming the people around them. This book is not about them, but, instead, about you. In it, I focus on how to take care of yourself during and after a relationship with someone who treats you with unkindness or abuse, exploits you, and erodes your self-worth and sanity. You will find many books and websites that can help you understand your toxic partner's pathology, and you will have a long time to contemplate this difficult relationship and your vulnerability to it in the future. Right now, if you are ready to think about reasons to exit, to make a plan for exiting, to execute that plan, and to recover from the pain connected to this relationship, the practices in this book will prepare you to move forward and into your best life.

Before we move on, I offer two technical notes about the book:

First, I use the concept of "personality disorder" here as a kind of shorthand for clusters of challenging behaviors that show up in intimate relationships because many people — clinicians, partners, and psychotherapy clients — know and use this concept and it allows us a common frame of reference. Unlike some clinicians and lay people, however, I do not believe that these clusters of behaviors are impervious to change. My own perspective is that these problematic behavioral styles are rooted in trauma, disrupted attachment experiences, and cultural factors; I believe people with these patterns and styles can heal, change, and grow. To do so requires deep commitments, courage, and motivation, along with skillful therapeutic support.

The possibility that folks with narcissistic, "borderline," and anti-social traits can heal and change doesn't mean that your particular partner can make that journey right now or that you should stay with the hope that they will wake up because of your love or support. Indeed, your relationship dynamics with them may completely reinforce their most difficult traits and patterns, so ending your relationship with them not only benefits you but shows compassion toward them, no matter how they view it at present. The fact that we can trace someone's unskillful behavior to their history of trauma, neglect, or poor parenting does not relieve them of responsibility for that behavior. If you're being treated poorly, have explored various strategies for shifting the dynamic, and have been rewarded with no significant change, leaving may be the best course of action you can take for yourself – and for your partner.

Second, you'll also notice that instead of using singular masculine and feminine pronouns — "he" and "she"— I use the English pronoun "they" in places you would usually see the singular. I do this for two reasons related to inclusivity. First, not everyone identifies with the pronouns "he" and "she," preferring instead a range of alternatives beyond that binary, including "they." Second, the classic literature on personality disorders usually assumes narcissistic and anti-social people are men and people with Borderline Personality Disorder (BPD) traits are women, an inaccurate over-simplification resulting in resources divided by gender (books for men about "borderline" wives, books for women about narcissistic husbands, and few resources for people with the inverse situation or in same-sex relationships). This book addresses the needs of people working

4

through difficult relationships with partners who have extremely challenging traits across categories of sex, gender, sexual identity, and "diagnosis." Across these variations, the dynamics are remarkably similar — as are the steps and skills you need to exit and to recover. Whatever the details of your toxic relationship may be, if you have come to the conclusion that exiting is worth serious consideration, I hope you will find *The Five Step Exit* a clear roadmap for your journey.

CONTEMPLATION

Contemplation is the first step of *The Five Step Exit*.

Here, at the beginning, it's important to contemplate your situation. At its most simplistic, "contemplation" refers to thinking something over. "Contemplation" carries deeper meanings, however, and it's the deeper practice of contemplation I hope to help you cultivate here.

You may be very bright, have a good education, and have strong skills when it comes to thinking your way through problems in many areas of life. In a toxic relationship, however, thinking can get in the way of clarity.

Unlike other situations you face regularly or problems you have solved in the past, your toxic relationship involves elements that complicate the process of simply thinking it through to come to a clear conclusion. Toxic relationships keep people in states of emotional agitation. They raise what seem to be moral and ethical questions different from those in healthy relationships. They cultivate addiction to the relationship and to the toxic partner, and create logistical traps and no-win situations.

Simply thinking in the face of these circumstances leads to many dead ends; you may already feel that you are running through a maze with no exit as you try to think your way out of your toxic relationship.

We know that there exist many kinds of intelligence. Rational problem solving, creative improvisation, and innovation will serve you very well as you exit your toxic relationship, but beneath these, in the deeper places of wisdom and knowing, you will find the guidance that will help you create a clear sense of direction and a commitment to moving forward.

In many traditions, people connect the concept of contemplation to a sense of the sacred. Whether you identify with an institutionalized religion, consider yourself spiritual but not religious, or think of yourself as an atheist, a sense of the sacred is available to you. Contemplating your difficult relationship situation while listening to your truest sense of aliveness will help you move from ruminating relentlessly on the hamster wheel of "thinking" and toward taking skillful action that respects your own well-being.

Contemplation transcends thinking and uses the knowledge of your body, the wisdom of your experience, and the connection of your life to the greater universe to move you toward insight on the best course of action.

I've designed the practices in this section of the book to help you become ever more clear about what you need to do to have your best life possible and to be your best possible self in a world that needs each of us to help heal it in our own ways. If you are uncertain about leaving, these exercises should help you get clearer about whether leaving is the right choice.

If a contemplative experience has already offered a sacred insight that you need to exit, I encourage you to do these exercises anyway. Ambiguity is the heart of drama; clarity is the heart of peace. Contemplation will help you reduce ambiguity and set out on the right path for you with courage, commitment, and grace.

Making shift happen

You've heard the old saying about the difficulty fish have in noticing the water they swim in. When you are in a toxic relationship, the polluted water you are swim in begins to seem normal. Your ideas about how you should be treated reflect the noxious status quo in the relationship. Some of this may be because you have not always been treated well in relationships in the past. I know of women who have talked to their mothers about being emotionally abused by their husbands, only to hear their mothers say, "at least he isn't beating you like your Dad beat me."

Sometimes, your standards shift because the your partner has slowly worn away the habits that used to seem normal to you in relationships — they have groomed you to accept unkind speech or being ignored or having no input into the choices that affect your household.

Sometimes, you have made a conscious choice to continue in the relationship knowing that you don't like how the other person treats you because it seems easier to roll with the toxic stuff than to get out for one reason or another—money, kids, social status, fear of loneliness.

Still, what you're being exposed to takes its toll on your self-esteem, on your dreams, on your creativity, on your ability to feel confident about making things happen in your life, and perhaps on your financial, practical, and material welfare as well.

Your perspective needs to change.

In this practice, which will serve you well in all kinds of relationships and through all phases of ending a relationship with a toxic person, you will come up with a new standard for the behaviors and treatment you expect and accept from others.

First, imagine someone in your life from whom you felt unconditional love and acceptance. This could be a grandparent, a teacher, a friend, a child you love, even a companion animal like a dog or cat or horse with whom you felt a close attachment. It could be a religious figure or teacher you admire and feel some connection with. If you can't recall ever feeling loved and accepted in this way, find an example that appeals to you in the relationships among your friends, neighbors, or co-workers — one in which you see people treating each other well, one in which you can't imagine either person behaving as your partner does. Jackson Mackenzie, author of the excellent book *Psychopath Free* (2015), calls the mental image of this loving presence your "Constant," because you can use your knowledge of how this person or being would want you to be treated in every situation to set a standard – they consistently want the best for you.

Second, spend some time thinking about how your Constant would view the dynamics in your relationship. Would they feel sad or angry? Would they feel the urge to protect you or to remove you from your situation? If your partner yells at you or lies to you, would your Constant be comfortable with this? The goal here is not to bring up shame around this relationship, but to get in touch with a frame of reference that helps you evaluate what is acceptable to you. If your Constant would not feel happy about the behavior, it's behavior that shouldn't be acceptable to you either. In the context of toxic relationships, we often lose sight of our right to be treated well. The Constant reminds us that all of us deserve to be treated with kindness, care, dignity, and respect in our most intimate relationships.

You may want to put a picture of your Constant someplace that allows you to take a glance at their image on a regular basis. If it helps, you can imagine your Constant in the room with you during difficult interactions with your partner. Imagine whether you would be comfortable having this interaction in front of your Constant, and how your Constant would respond if they observed it.

When you doubt whether what your person did or said is normal, okay, or acceptable, call up the image of your Constant. Imagine your Constant's name on one of those "What Would Xena Do?" bumper stickers: "Would my Constant be cool with this?" If the answer is no, you need to think about how to respond in a way that signals that you will not accept the behavior, either.

Naming snakes

It's important to see clearly the kinds of pain and damage your partner has created for you. When you feel tempted to think things will improve if you continue or return, having an inventory of the heartaches they have caused can support your clarity and decision making.

Most likely, your toxic partner consciously or unconsciously has used "intermittent reinforcement" — sometimes attentive, responsive, amazing, kind/sometimes absent, distant, thoughtless, cruel — to hook you. When things hurt, your memories of more pleasant experiences with this person at other times can keep you hopeful that you will "get your real partner" back. Unfortunately, the behavior you have experienced from them in the past is the behavior you will experience in the future, if you stay or return. It is vitally important that you see your partner clearly.

Various cultural traditions have stories, myths, and sayings that encourage us to be aware of self-deception about the nature of others who might harm us. One story describes a lonely peasant woman who takes pity on a small snake in her garden. She brings the snake inside, feeds it, allows it to live under her warm stove, and daily talks to the snake to meet her own needs for companionship. After some time, the snake reaches maturity, thanks to the nurturing of the woman. One morning, the woman comes into the kitchen and greets her companion, who bites her, injecting her with poisonous venom. As she writhes in pain, about to die, the woman says "Snake, I have given you only kindness! Why did you bite me? Why are you killing me?" The snake responds, "I am a snake. It is in my nature to bite and kill. You knew I was a snake when you brought me in."

For this practice, I would like you to put aside all of the "amazing/unforgettable/incredible" moments you have had with your partner, and focus exclusively on the concerning moments.

I would like you to start a list. Think back to before your romance began. Were there concerns for you then? List those. Include any reservations you may have had about how they behaved while in another relationship. Now begin to list issues, events, and concerns during your own involvement with this person. Include incidents in which they have lied to, cheated on, financially exploited, "blown off," verbally abused, deceived, manipulated, or humiliated you, or put you into no-win situations. Don't forget situations in which they expected you to compromise your values or pressured or demeaned you if you established certain boundaries. Include multiple break-ups, if you have been through them, and what led up to them.

It's okay to start the list and add to it over several days. Sometimes, in toxic relationships, things happen so quickly that we don't have time to process particular events very well; sometimes, we don't realize until later that we have been conned. Starting these lists often begins to open the door to a backlog of memories of hurtful or outrageous incidents. As your memories of these surface, put them on the list.

When you feel the list is fairly complete, identify the ten most painful things that have happened in your relationship with your toxic partner.

Transfer your 'top ten" to an index card for your wallet or to a sticky note for your car dash; if you have a cell phone, send yourself a text message with the top ten. If you spend a lot of time in other places put the top ten list there, too.

Any time you find yourself feeling tempted to remain, or to go back to your Ex, or feel down about the relationship ending, review the top ten list. You did not fabricate these incidents, and they demonstrate the nature of the person with whom you are dealing. Although snakes have many beautiful, magical, fascinating, amazing, qualities, many of them are very dangerous to human beings — poisonous ones can do much damage with only one bite. If you are dealing with a poisonous person, you will be wise to remember their nature and to keep yourself out of harm's way.

Turn down the volume. Look at the screen.

Although we live in a very visual culture, we sometimes allow what we hear to over-ride what we see and experience when we are in toxic relationships. We may feel mistreated; we may see our partner or lover take actions that we find confusing, distressing, or disturbing. Nonetheless, if the person tells you that they love you, are totally into you or committed to your relationship, and/or that they want to change, you may make the mistake of trusting what they say instead of trusting your own observations and experience. It would be lovely if your partner were someone whose word were reliable and whose track record confirmed that what they say lines up with how they act. If that were the case, however, you wouldn't feel so exhausted, distressed, crazy, and demoralized. In healthy relationships, things line up. In unhealthy relationships, the disconnect between what people say and what they do is a fertile field for manipulation, gas-lighting (intentional deception that leaves the deceived person feeling or looking crazy), and exploitation.

In this practice, imagine that you can observe your relationship on a large movie screen. The movie you are watching is a silent movie. Run across the screen in your mind scenes in which you met, scenes in which you felt happy and valued, scenes in which things seemed to be going wrong. Pay attention to the patterns you see — for example, were all of the good times a result of efforts you made to create a nice experience without any effort or contribution on your partner's part? Do all of the good times involve drinking or drugs? Do all of the good times happen when you spend money on things that benefit your partner, or is there reciprocity? Do you see your partner "playing" two people at once? Pay attention to your actions and to your partner's. When you turn down the volume and only look at the screen, are you seeing a romance, a mystery, a thriller, a porn film, a tragedy, or a documentary about a con artist? What surprises you? Do you see your partner failing to show up for an important occasion without notice or apology and then see yourself continuing to show up for them, maybe even redoubling your efforts to engage? Without a soundtrack, as you watch your own behavior, imagine how you would interpret this if you saw it in a stranger.

If you are still involved with the toxic person in your life or are at risk of re-engaging, begin to observe their behaviors as though you were watching them on film, no matter what they are saying. In normal relationships, we can put great stock in what partners say because their behaviors generally support their actions. In toxic relationships, partners are often deceived not by behaviors but by what sociopaths, narcissists, and people with borderline personality disorders say — the smokescreens they create, the excuses they make, the sad tales they tell to engage your sympathy and keep you in the game. By turning down the volume and focusing carefully on the screen — *and then responding to the behavior rather than to the story* — you will become clearer, wiser, and stronger in how you respond to people toxic to you.

Envision your future self

Some research in the social sciences says that our visions of our futures shape our current decisions. If we allow ourselves to be confused and exhausted by the drama of the present, we may not have much time or energy to consider how what is happening now could narrow our options or our wellbeing in the future. While there are many, many advantages to being present in the current moment, we do ourselves a disservice if we don't allow ourselves to contemplate how the present will have consequences down the line.

When you are in a relationship with a toxic person, it makes sense to expect that what you have seen so far in their behavior will continue. If you have experienced crazy-making instability, financial exploitation, cheating, lying, or other kinds of abusive behaviors from your partner, you will experience these again in the future, even if things are calm at the moment.

Imagine what your life will look life if you continue to include in it a person who behaves the way your toxic partner behaves. Imagine yourself one year, two years, five years, and ten years in the future, after one, two, five, and ten more years of drama, exploitation, and heartache. How do you envision your health? Your mental health? Your friendships? The welfare of your family members? Your finances? Your career? Your ability to have in life what you would like to have?

If you happen to know (from direct experience or observation, not from your Ex's representations) anything about the people with whom your Ex has been involved in the past, take into account how well they doing. Do they look older than their years? Do they have many health problems? Have they experienced financial trouble? Your toxic partner may tell you that their Exes are crazy, abusive, alcoholic, financial disasters. It is important to question the truth of this, as well as the extent to which the Exes' current problems have roots in what they experienced with your mate.

Now imagine your life in the future if you can free yourself from the toxic relationship. Envision your health, your mental health, and your friendships. Envision your career, your finances, and your ability to concentrate on having the experiences or things you want in life. What would your life look like in one, two, five, and ten years? While it may be bumpy early in a separation from a disordered person, the further out on the horizon you can envision, the more you can probably see yourself having an active, happy, peaceful, and interesting life. It even has room in it for a person who can reciprocate your attention, affection, and generosity, and with whom you can move forward toward common dreams.

Focus on your ideal future. Make choices in this moment — and the next, and the next — that allow you to lay the foundation for a happy, expansive life. Each moment you spend mired in a toxic relationship is a moment of your present and future happiness and wellbeing that you sacrifice.

Meditate on the question

Even if your experiences before now have not included a formal introduction to meditation, I can assure you that you have transferable skills – and that meditating will serve you well as you contemplate the question of leaving. You have very likely experienced something like meditation, and have also likely experienced some of the benefits that more purposeful meditation can provide.

One of the natural meditation skills you already possess is the ability to breathe, to inhale and exhale. Another is to pay attention. In meditation, as we pay attention to the breath, breathing in, breathing out, we can help ourselves become more centered. As we are more centered, we are calmer, know our feelings better, and become able to think and perceive things more clearly.

You may have experienced states similar to those produced by meditation through religious practices such as prayer; you may also have experienced them in situations requiring intense focus that engages your mind, body, and spirit. People often have these moments in activities requiring a great deal of attention to the breath, such as swimming, running, biking, rock climbing, dancing, singing or chanting with others, and making love. Through these activities, we often feel very alive, present, and centered. Meditative states often involve similar feelings of peace and vibrancy; it's important to know that you can create this experience for yourself through meditation –no half marathon required!– and that it can be helpful to you.

There exist many forms of meditation; sometimes we use meditation for the simple, single purpose of becoming more centered; sometimes we use meditation to study our own minds, understanding that our minds have habits that may or may not be helpful to us and that we can change, once we have become more familiar with them; sometimes we use meditation to work with our tendency to view ourselves as separate and alone, and to cultivate deeper understandings of our interconnectedness and to nurture lovingkindness — both toward others and ourselves.

If you are experienced in meditation, all of this may be very familiar territory. If meditation is new to you, please don't worry about "getting it right" or needing to know the many different approaches to meditation that have come to the West in the last half century from Eastern traditions. You can learn more about that as your meditation practice deepens, if it interests you. Whether you are experienced with meditation or have never meditated before, I've designed the following practice for you at this particular moment in your life, as you contemplate ending your toxic relationship.

The Steps:

1. Find a pleasant location where you will be undisturbed for a few minutes. Consider being outside, though inside will work just fine, too.
2. Sit in a way that is comfortable for you, with your spine elongated and your chin slightly elevated. You may sit on the ground, on the floor, or on a chair that provides some support for sitting with good posture. Allow your hands to rest lightly on your legs. You may fold your hands in your lap or allow each hand to rest, palm up, on your thighs.
3. Soften your gaze so that you allow your eyelids to become a little heavy and allow your vision to go into "soft focus," looking at the ground or floor slightly ahead of your body. If you are comfortable, you can close your eyes completely.
4. Begin to inhale deeply and slowly through your nose, focusing on expanding your belly with each in-breath. Exhale slowly through your mouth. Continue breathing in this way, mindful of your upright posture, until you feel yourself become a little more relaxed.
5. As you relax, continue breathing slowly, and drop your consciousness below your body; envision that your "energy body" extends a few feet in all directions around you, including into the earth below; now begin to envision your breath extending into the bottom of your energy body as you inhale, and envision the energy of the earth rising through your body as you exhale.
6. Continue this practice until you feel yourself relax a little more.
7. As you continue to breathe in this way, ask yourself the question: "What is the most loving way for me to treat myself in this situation?"
8. Continue to breathe deeply into your energy body, allowing the greater energy to flow up through your feet and into your solar plexus as you exhale, as you continue to contemplate this question.
9. As answers to the question arise, allow them to come into your consciousness; note them; then release them. Make space for the arising of as many answers as come. If no

answer comes, that's okay too.

10. Continue to breathe deeply and to return to the question, "What is the most loving way for me to treat myself in this situation?" for a few more minutes.

11. When you feel relaxed and ready, open your eyes, return to a normal gaze, center your breathing in the middle of your solar plexus, and stretch your body.

12. Allow yourself to stay relaxed as long as possible; review the thoughts that came to you as you contemplated the question, "What is the most loving way for me to treat myself in this situation?"

13. If the answer to the question is "the most loving thing for me to do for myself is to remove myself from this situation," trust it, and know that the next step is to begin to prepare.

PREPARATION

To end your toxic relationship as safely, quickly, and successfully as possible, you will need to have a plan of action, an exit plan. The practices in this section of the book will help you prepare yourself to leave by making that plan.

Preparation is the second step of *The Five Step Exit*.

If you are like many people in toxic relationships, your emotional resources have been depleted by frequent "surprises" and extreme demands that keep you un-centered, on-guard, and exhausted. You find it difficult to make plans for the weekend, let alone plans for dinner, because your partner is predictably unpredictable, controlling, and skilled at undermining you. Making an exit plan will help restore some of your sense of control over your own life, help you feel empowered to take the risks involved in leaving, and help you take the next step toward reclaiming your future. It will also give you a blueprint for exiting that will keep you safer, reduce the drama of the process, and allow you to feel good and guilt-free about how you handle the exit.

Toxic relationships have common dynamics but a wide range of circumstances. In extreme situations, people face physical violence or restrictions on their freedom to leave their homes or contact friends, family, and police. Exiting other situations may involve financial risk, downward mobility, threats of retaliation, and drama that will drag on for awhile. Sometimes, when we're fortunate, ending a toxic relationship simply does come down to telling the other person that things are over. If you don't live together, don't have financial involvements or kids, and the person will be offended enough by your rejection that they won't contact you again, consider yourself fortunate. Ultimately, only you know the details and dynamics of your particular situation, so you are in the best position to determine what kind of exit plan to make and how to set it in motion when the time comes. I've designed the practices in this section of the book to help you use the information you already have about your toxic partner, your relationship dynamic, and your strengths and vulnerabilities to do the practical and emotional work of getting ready to exit. Knowledge can, indeed, be leveraged as power. The practices in this section will help you think calmly and clearly about how to use what you know to create the most effective exit possible and to lay the foundations for the better life ahead of you.

Design your dream team

As you leave your toxic relationship, you will need support. It is predictable that circumstances will get bumpy at times along the way, and you will face a range of emotional challenges that may include pressure to reconcile, threats from your ex, and handling difficult logistical and financial issues. Sometimes, you will need sympathetic listeners. Sometimes, you will need "tough love" reminders about why you have decided to leave and the positive possibilities leaving will create for you. Sometimes you will need expertise that you yourself don't have. As you prepare to end the relationship, an important practice is to put together your Dream Team, the network of resources that will help you navigate a steady course toward your dream of a more peaceful, productive, creative life.

Many of your friends and family members will be supportive of your decision to leave. You may have had friends say to you that they can't be around you while you are in the throes of your toxic relationship. Although you may have felt abandoned when they made this decision, letting them know of your preparations to get out will likely be welcome news. Those friends will be happy to support you. It's important that as you prepare to leave, you share this information only with people you trust not to share it with others, including your significant other. Gossip among members of your social network will complicate your efforts to end the relationship and possibly put you at risk of harm. Seek support among trustworthy friends who have a track record of reliability and the capacity to keep confidences.

Do not share your plans with your partner's people.

You may be tempted to do this out of a kind impulse toward your Ex, hoping relatives or caregivers will check on them, take care of them, etc., if they engage in high-risk behavior as the breakup unfolds. Resist this temptation; it is important for you to relinquish your role as your partner's caretaker, and to reduce the risk that third parties will complicate your efforts to exit. Use your support system, not the other person's.

What can your friends and family do? Beyond moral support, friends and family may be able to help with a range of practical needs. As you end the relationship, friends and family can check on your welfare and safety or that of your children or pets, if things become volatile at home. You may find yourself needing a temporary place to stay during the exit process, and friends may be able to offer a couch or a spare bedroom while the dust settles. Most importantly, friends can remind you of your best self, why you need to leave, and that there is a better life ahead of you if you can stay on track.

Depending on your circumstances, you may need the help, counsel, and skills of a range of professionals. Let's talk about some of the possible players for you to consider recruiting to your team.

Therapists and Counselors. Many people benefit from discussing their exit plan with a therapist or counselor who has worked with personality disordered people and their partners. A therapist with skills in this area can validate your reasons for leaving, help you anticipate challenges that may come up, and prepare to respond skillfully when your significant other "acts out" in the process of the break-up. Cultivating this relationship before you actually end things with your spouse, partner, or lover allows you and the therapist to build rapport and trust, so that if you need consultation in an emergency, you know who to call and trust their guidance, confident that the therapist knows the history of your relationship. If you don't have a therapist or counselor already, make sure to ask those you consider hiring if they have had experience working with people with personality disorders or their partners.

Attorneys and Legal Advisors. You may also need legal advice. If you live with your toxic mate in a marriage or legal domestic partnership, or as two single adults, meet with an attorney or someone else familiar with local housing ordinances regarding your legal rights and obligations and the other party's. If the two of you own a home or other property together, co-own a business, or share retirement accounts, or if you are entitled to your partner's savings, worry that your partner will lay claim to yours, or have children, consulting an attorney can be invaluable.

Sometimes, even if you aren't married and don't live together, you may need legal counsel if your former date or lover decides they will make your life miserable. You do have legal protections from slander and libel, stalking, harassment, and a host of other kinds of unwanted and harmful behaviors. In some situations, your need for counsel will be on-going. Sometimes, a strongly worded letter from an attorney conveying to the other person that you intend not to tolerate abusive behavior and will take legal action if it continues puts a stop to harassment or defamation.

Law Enforcement. Unfortunately, you may need to have contact with local police at some point during your separation process. Fortunately, law enforcement can often serve as a valuable resource. Officers in your area can let you know how they see your right of access and your partner's access to any home you share, and can advise you on how to respond to difficult situations in which your partner is unreasonable or demanding. If you are concerned about your Ex breaking into your home or coming in without the right to be there, or if you are being stalked, advising your local police department can be very helpful. Often, officers will give additional attention to what's happening at your residence. They also may talk directly with your Ex, letting them know that their behavior risks crossing a legal line and advising them to stop. If your Ex does cross that line, you may file for a restraining order that legally directs them to avoid certain behaviors or risk jail time. If they engage in harassment, physical violence, threats of violence, property damage, child endangerment, or stalking, they can be arrested.

Many of us resist seeking help from the police, especially if we come from communities that have a history of difficult relationships with law enforcement, as do people of color, gay, lesbian, and trans folks, and people born in other countries. Nonetheless, being proactive in contacting the police about concerns you anticipate arising can be helpful. It allows you greater influence over the situation than if you contact police only in the heat of a dangerous or difficult interaction.

Crisis Intervention Specialists. If your partner has a history of self-injury, suicide attempts, or suicide threats, you may find yourself dealing with this during your separation. Having a plan for this, including knowing who to call if your Ex threatens or attempts suicide, can be very helpful. In addition to calling your local law enforcement agency or emergency response medical team — essentially 9-1-1 in the US — you may also want to know how to reach the local mental health crisis response team. We will talk more about this later in the book, but for now it's important to note that if your Ex makes a suicide threat or attempt, your best response will be to call police and medical responders and the local crisis unit, rather than to engage in drama, negotiations, or direct intervention yourself. There will come a day when you will know that the absolute best response to a toxic partner threatening suicide is to say "I am sorry you're at risk. Knowing that, I need to ask professionals to step in."

Respite Care-givers for Kids and Animals. If you have children or animals, they need to be prioritized in any plan you make. During the breakup/separation/divorce process, consider where the children and pets will be safest, feel most secure and peaceful, and be exposed to as little craziness as possible. If you and your partner live together with your children, you may be tempted to leave the home in the breakup. Only do this after careful consideration of the impact on your kids. Will your Ex abuse them because you can no longer be a target? Will they attempt suicide with children in the house? Will the legal system consider you to have "abandoned the home," putting you in a vulnerable situation when it comes to custody and property issues? If you take your child with you, will you be accused of kidnapping? As you inform friends and others about your effort to end the relationship, identify people who may be willing to have the children or pets stay with them if circumstances at home become so dramatic or challenging that you are concerned about their welfare.

Financial Advisors. Finally, you may need a financial advisor. To the extent that you can, begin to separate your finances, assets, joint property, and shared resources, such as health insurance, prior to the breakup or separation. If you have large sums of money to protect, consult a financial advisor, accountant, and lawyer. Some financial experts specialize in "forensic accounting," and provide investigations of situations in which a spouse may be hiding money.

Often, you can access free resources that can be helpful at a financial institution, such as a bank or credit union; financial advisors there can assist in segregating joint accounts, taking the other party off of your lines of credit, and helping you begin to prepare for your financial life beyond the present. If you will be in debt or at a financial deficit as a result of this relationship, it is better to look the situation squarely in the face, stop the drain on your resources now, and begin to make a plan for rebuilding. The sooner you start, the sooner you will be done!

Name your priorities

As you prepare to end your relationship with a personality disordered person for the final time — literally for good — it is important to recognize that while the long range forecast of your life will improve in many ways following a final break, the short term could present some challenging weather. If you were preparing for a natural disaster, you would think carefully about your priorities. If you were going to evacuate your home, what would you take with you? What would be most important for your wellbeing and happiness going forward? You need to apply similar thinking to your exit plan for this relationship.

What are your priorities? What is at risk? What are you willing to sacrifice? What needs to be protected?

Spend some time now thinking about the places that you feel vulnerable in this relationship, and the ways your disordered partner could interfere with your well-being in its aftermath. For example, your partner may owe you money that you have a right to pursue through legal channels. Are you willing to sacrifice it, or is it a priority to be compensated for it? If having your money returned is important, consider what you will sacrifice by pursuing it through legal channels. Time? Legal expenses? Difficulty in moving on?

Make an inventory of what is important to you in your life at present, with an eye toward the future. Make a written list of your priorities. You will use this list as you plan and when things get stormy as you move toward a final exit, however long that may take.

Limit your priorities to five, and assign numbers to them in rank order, so that you can be clear about your greatest priority on the list. In the future, if things become turbulent, you will ask yourself "What is the relationship between the current drama and my top five? What do I need to do to protect my top five priorities during this current crisis?"

A list might look like this:

1. Keeping my job
2. Keeping a car
3. Making progress toward my degree
4. Protecting my nest egg
5. Getting sleep

Notice that on this person's list, keeping a job is of primary importance, but housing doesn't show up. If you asked her about this, she might say, "I have a mortgage, but I am willing to lose the house; as long as I have a job, I know I can keep a roof over my head, and whether I own it or not is not my highest priority. Digging out will take some time, so I need to protect my job, my education, the car I drive to get to these places, and the small nest egg I have in savings. I am not getting good sleep, so that is also on my top five. I am committed not to making any big decisions when I am sleep deprived because I know this is a way that my person wears me down."

If you saw this list, with the items ranked in this order, what questions would you ask about these priorities? Should sleep be first, rather than last (even though it is still in the top five)?

Make your own list now. Play around with the items on it until you can identify your top five. Discuss the list with a couple of close friends who are aware of your situation and your plan to end your toxic relationship. Ask for their feedback, questions, and recommendations. Adjust as makes sense.

Write your final list down and put it in your wallet, on your electronic device, in a file with your paperwork related to your exit, on your car dash, on your desk, etc.

When things become hectic, chaotic, dramatic, frightening, or confusing, use your priorities as a guide for protecting the things that are important and letting go of issues, things, and dramas that will not support you in pursuing your priorities.

Powerful predicting

You have been with this person long enough to have a sense of their modus operandi, how they respond when they don't get their way, how they respond when they feel rejected or offended. In this practice, you will use what you know about your significant other to predict how the person will react when you move forward with your freedom.

How did your person end other relationships or respond to someone ending a relationship with them? Think about their behavior not only in other romantic relationships but also in work and family relationships.

What have been the dynamics in your relationship around these key issues?

1. Violence and safety
2. Independence and autonomy
3. Control of money
4. Childcare and parental decision making, if you have kids
5. Dramas involving other people
6. Crazy accusations
7. Lying or misrepresentations
8. Bargaining or resisting change in unhealthy ways

If your partner has been violent with you during your relationship, you will be in greater danger of being on the receiving end of violence during the breakup.

If you know or suspect that your partner has a history of violence, even if they have never been violent with you, expect that in the trajectory of your breakup, their inhibitions against using violence with you will disappear and you will be a target. If your partner tells you stories about others being violent with them that now make little sense to you, contemplate whether these stories are projections (something they did that they say someone else did) or twisted versions of the truth designed to make them look better if you discover they were violent with someone else.

If your partner has made suicide attempts —even if it was long ago — or threatened to suicide at times of stress in your relationship, you should predict that this is a possibility now.

If your partner has exploited you financially or limited your access to money or been unreliable about settling debts with you or contributing to common expenses, do not expect them to be financially fair in a break-up. If you know that your partner has been involved in ugly financial or legal battles during other breakups, expect them to try to engage in financial and legal combat with you as you leave. This might include simply refusing to resolve unfinished financial business in order to leave you struggling, trying to freeze shared assets, refusing to make payments on property or possessions held in common in order to hurt your bank account, destroy your credit, and aggravate you, or suing you for support, even if you were not married and have been underwriting their expensive habits all along. Use what information you already have to predict the extent to which your person will or will not play fairly as you work to regain your autonomy.

Use what you know from your relationship and from what your partner has said about previous relationships to predict the future during your breakup. If, early in your relationship with your partner, they presented themselves as a sympathetic victim of their last partner, read between the lines of that early story to figure out what really might have happened. Expect your future Ex to be telling a similar story starring you in the near future, as he or she works on reeling the next victim in.

Use what you know to predict how this will go.

Worst case scenarios

As you prepare to end your toxic relationship, your mind may run wild with frightening possibilities: "What if she kills herself?" "What if he stalks me?" "What if they ruin me in my workplace?"

Instead of dismissing these possibilities or minimizing them, in this practice I ask you to indulge them. In fact, I am going to ask you to make them even more elaborate and fantastic than they already are. And then, I am going to ask you to answer back in a powerful way. Rather than allowing your mind to disable you with fear, we are going to start to come up with a response plan for every worry that arises. I am going to teach you to plan for a Worst Case Scenario.

Frightening things happen in our world. Tornados. Hurricanes. Blizzards. Tsunamis. Earthquakes. Fires. Ebola outbreaks. Horrible flu seasons. Terrorist attacks. Active shooter situations. As a crisis worker, I know that communities, businesses, and social service organizations, along with county, state, and federal governments, develop crisis response plans that include communication systems, people who can be called in on short notice to help and who are specially trained in responding to particular aspects of a crisis (from mental health workers, to animal specialists, to firefighters and EMS, to security people, blood donor coordinators, and communications specialists, etc.), evacuation routes, emergency supplies and funds, and plans for housing people who are suddenly without safe, secure places to stay. Your toxic relationship has probably been an ongoing personal disaster. As you prepare to leave, it makes sense to use the planning skills of disaster response workers to prepare yourself for the final hurrah.

So, what is your worst-case-breakup-scenario in this moment?

Imagine this: you come home to discover your living space gutted, your credit cards missing, your animals hiding in fear, suicide threats scrawled on your walls, and the police waiting for you. The police have been called by your Ex, who has reported that you have created this chaos and will kill yourself. Your Ex has hacked your e-mail and Facebook accounts and sent disturbing messages to loved ones and colleagues. Your Ex has asked the police to detain you for mental health reasons and has announced they are going into hiding because they are afraid of you. They've been very convincing. Tomorrow, you are scheduled to leave town for an important family reunion, to go to court to finalize the adoption of your child, to go to the university to defend your dissertation, or to start a new job, which, of course, they know.

If you faced this scenario, what choices would you make to take care of your life and your goals? How would you respond to the police? How would you address the issue of missing credit cards? How would you deal with the mess? Where would you go for the night? What are the most important actions for you to take to make sure you are where you need to be in the morning? How would you respond to your Ex, and on what timeline?

If you can plan to address this extreme scenario and others more relevant to you, you will be prepared for nearly anything that happens. Remember to use as a point of reference the five priorities that you have already identified earlier in this section.

I share these possibilities to prepare you, not to scare you.

Through careful preparation for ending a toxic relationship, you will be able to respond with clarity and calm if there are a few explosions over the course of your five step exit from a toxic relationship. The fact that there is some real risk of this kind of drama tells you how toxic your relationship has become, and how important it is for your health and happiness that you get out.

Mental rehearsal

As a graduate student, I worked for the Rape Education and Prevention Program (REPP) at Ohio State University. The amazing women who trained me to teach practical self-defense also taught me the power of using mental rehearsal to respond to our anxieties and fears.

For example, if you fear your Ex will show up at your workplace, you could review this scenario repeatedly in your mind, making yourself increasingly anxious. Using positive mental rehearsal as an alternative, you allow the image to come up but then move forward into images of yourself responding to this situation from a centered and creative space. If your Ex comes to your workplace, imagine simply refusing to come out when you learn you have an uninvited visitor. "I'm in a meeting," you might say. Or imagine coming into the lobby and repeating only, "You need to leave now." Or imagine stepping away and calmly calling security. Or imagine noticing your Ex in the parking lot, turning, and going inside to report this trespassing to police. Imagine allowing your Ex to rant and rave while you calmly observe, without reactivity or fear, recognizing that this behavior only reflects on them, not on you.

There are many ways you can respond effectively to each possible situation that may begin to worry you. By meeting the anxious scenarios that come up as you plan to exit with visions of the creative, skillful responses you will take, you put your fears and anxieties into their proper proportions. Along the way, you prepare yourself to respond calmly and effectively to any drama your Ex creates, up to and including your Worst Case Scenario.

Develop a detailed exit strategy

Decide how, when, and where to deliver your decision and your plan for addressing any unresolved issues between you and your partner. In healthy relationships that offer us emotional safety, having a direct, face-to-face conversation with a date, partner, or spouse about ending a relationship is the responsible and caring approach. It is often different with people who have personality disorders. If your significant other repeatedly distorts reality to manipulate others, you may wish to put your decision to end the relationship in writing. You cannot control how this will be shared, but you can control the language you use and the message you send. By writing to them, you also are creating a record that may be useful to you later, if your Ex accuses you of saying things that you did not, or if documenting some elements of the ending becomes significant legally in the future.

Some people decide that they will be safest if they inspire their toxic partner to leave them; many who attempt to use this strategy, however, discover their toxic partners difficult to manipulate into a break-up.

In general, I recommend making a careful, active plan that puts you back into the driver's seat of your own life. Your toxic partner may accuse you of trying to control them, or of being a bully, when, of course, they have been controlling and bullying you throughout the relationship. Your goal here is not to control them, but to be free of their control, and to once again become centered in and responsible for your own life.

If you live together, you will need a timeline for separating your possessions and moving to separate living spaces. If your significant other is a squatter in your home, determine a date by which they need to be out. If the home belongs to your partner, make a plan for when you will move out and all of the steps that need to be coordinated to make that happen. If there are no children involved, do as much of the groundwork as possible for your exit before discussing the breakup with your significant other. If you are both on the deed or the lease, determine before you approach them about the break-up what your legal options are for terminating your mutual rights and obligations.

If you have been living together, or if they have a key to your place, plan to change the locks as soon as your legal rights allow. If you are moving, select your new place with security in mind. Rent a post office box so that your physical address is less available to the public. Make choices taking into account how easy it is for people to find information on-line about your address and phone number, and take measures to protect your privacy.

If you have joint banking or financial accounts, separate them as soon as you decide you will be exiting the relationship; end their access to your savings, checking, or credit card accounts as soon as it's legal for you to do this. Terminate joint accounts.

Take them off of your health and life insurance policies or get yourself off of theirs. When relationships that don't involve the dysfunctions associated with personality disorders end, these issues are often negotiated with thoughtfulness and care between partners or worked out by divorce attorneys. Unfortunately, in toxic relationships, informal agreements about these matters often fall apart when the disordered partner creates drama or fails to uphold their end of the agreement. Do your best to make sure you are taking care of your own interests. Don't act with the intention to harm the other person, but trust that they are more resourceful than you have assumed, and will find a way to address any problem created for them by the ending of the relationship.

Plan to terminate any marriage or domestic partnership you may have established. Take their name off of any accounts on which they may be a beneficiary as soon as it is legal for you to do so.

Change the passwords on your e-mail addresses, Facebook accounts, and bank accounts, even if you believe your partner doesn't know them or would never take advantage of them.

If you have joint property or possessions [vehicles, travel condos, campground sites, second homes or retreat spaces or land] consider whether you are willing to let these things go or how to assert your legal claims to them. If for some reason you have placed your assets in your partner's name alone, be prepared to lose them or explore, with an attorney, what would be involved with recovering them or their value.

If you are in the midst of achieving an important goal, such as having a child, finishing a degree, earning a promotion, landing your dream job, buying a home, undergoing a gender transition, attending a dying or ill parent, or launching your own business, expect that your Ex will attempt to manipulate you into sabotaging yourself. They will do this by creating drama at a critical point in the process. You must become exquisitely clear about your own commitment to your goals and priorities so that when the drama hits, you will be able to stay on track to achieving your plans. Return frequently to your priority list, your vision of your best life, and the practice of letting everything else go.

EXECUTION

Exiting a toxic relationship takes courage, commitment, and perseverance. It can be exhausting and, at times, frightening. The difficulties of the breakup reflect the difficulties of the relationship itself — frightening, crazy-making, exhausting. You have survived the relationship to this point; as you begin to act on the preparation and planning you've already done, it's important that you hold fast to the idea that you deserve to live in circumstances that are peaceful, with people who are kind and treat you well. By leaving your toxic relationship, you are opening the door to that possibility for yourself. It will be worth the challenge.

You've gotten in touch with the truth that you wouldn't allow someone to treat a person you love the way your significant other treats you and that if you are going to be kind to yourself, you need to remove yourself from this toxic situation. You've considered how your Ex might react — dramatically, vindictively, stoically — in response to your decision to end it, and you have done your best to prepare, emotionally, financially, and logistically for a worst case scenario. Now comes the moment when you accept that you have prepared as best you can and are ready to move forward to execute your plan. You know it will require some amount of improvisation and will likely be less than perfect at times but will, nonetheless, move you toward the life and the kinds of relationships you know you deserve.

Execution —taking action– is the third step of *The Five Step Exit*.

Timing can be a critical element of sharing with your significant other that you plan to exit your marriage or partnership or will not continue a dating relationship. Consider both your needs and those of the other person as you decide to share —or enact— your decision. Some people become very paralyzed with concern about breaking up close to one holiday or another, before or after a vacation, before or after an expensive date, before or after a birthday, before or after final exams, etc.

While it's important to take many variables into account as you prepare to have "the conversation," it's also important not to become so stymied by circumstances that you indefinitely postpone activating your exit plan.

There isn't really any particularly great time to end a relationship if your significant other isn't receptive to the idea. Take them into account, but try to focus on your needs as the ultimate guide for when to move forward. Some of the needs people have as they exit include: the need to be finished with the relationship; the need to stay safe; the need to have housing and access to resources such as money; the need to continue to work; and the need to avoid unnecessary drama.

Here are questions to consider as you move toward signaling that you intend to end the relationship:

1. Am I truly ready to commit to ending this toxic relationship? If my Ex pushes back, argues or bargains, cries and apologizes, blames me, or becomes charming, romantically or sexually, am I ready to resist the temptation to back down out of fear, obligation, guilt, or hopes that aren't grounded in reality?
2. If the relationship has been in a break-up/make-up cycle, have I done the work I need to do to prevent myself from continuing that pattern now? Have I taken actions to ensure this time will be different?
3. Have I put in place the plans and support systems I will need to resist any temptation to change course?
4. Have I done my best to protect my safety and that of children, pets, family members, and friends who could be hassled or harmed by my Ex in the wake of a breakup?
5. Do I have plans and strategies for staying in touch with my supports as the separation unfolds? Do I have back-up plans

for those plans? (For example, if my cell phone were destroyed, do I have a quick list of phone numbers of my emergency contacts stored somewhere safe?) Have I used what I know about my significant other's patterns of behavior to predict what might evolve in the breakup and to prepare for a worst case scenario?

When you are able to answer yes to these questions, you are in an excellent position to take the next step toward your freedom.

You may have decided you need to exit quickly and quietly while your significant other is at work or gone on a trip, if your safety will be threatened by staying in the house after you have announced your plan to end the relationship. You may have decided that you will sit down with your significant other and tell them directly that you need to end your relationship or, if there are kids involved, that you need to end your marriage or partnership even though your parenting responsibilities will continue. Perhaps you have decided to end the relationship in a therapist's office. Perhaps you have decided to send an e-mail message, so that your words are in written form because you want to begin to create a record of documentation about the dissolution. There is no one "right way" or "wrong way" for you to let the other person know your plan, just more and less skillful ways. By thinking things through ahead of time, as you have been doing, you have put yourself on the path to the most skillful exit you can create.

Be brave. This is one of the most difficult parts of the process of disconnecting from a toxic situation. You will feel much better when you have taken this next step, even if things become bumpy for awhile, because you will be gaining momentum. When you are as ready as you can be, use the planning and preparation you have done in the previous practices in this book to take the next step toward your freedom.

Skillful good-bye strategies

If you have decided to communicate your decision to end your toxic relationship directly to the other person, rather than making an exit without notice — which is indeed necessary in some cases — you have decisions to make about how and where to deliver your message. It's also important to be careful with the language you use. You will feel much better about yourself if you handle these conversations in ways that allow you to retain your dignity, stay centered, and stay clear and on message.

You know your situation and yourself better than anyone else, and you know your significant other, spouse, partner, or date well enough to have good expectations about how they will respond when you make your intentions clear. Using that awareness, you could decide to have this conversation in a number of ways:

- Face to face, in an environment where you feel safe
- Over the phone (not by text)
- In a letter
- By e-mail

In relationships with relatively healthy people, it's usually best simply to communicate face-to-face and directly, especially when you need to say something difficult. In toxic relationships, as you already have experienced, people regularly face volatility, aggression, gas-lighting (trying to convince you that you are out of touch with what's real), manipulation, lying, projection (accusing you of what they are doing), intimidation, bullying, and a host of challenging behaviors, even in the "good" times. In situations like these, give yourself permission to deliver the message in ways that you wouldn't in a relationship with someone who has treated you well. If you feel safer having the conversation by phone or sending an e-mail, it's okay to do so. Even if your significant other protests that it's unfair or disrespectful of you to convey the information this way, remember that you're allowed to share in a way that feels comfortable to you. The other person has an agenda that has already left you exhausted, confused, depleted, unhappy, and demoralized. If they object to how you are expressing yourself, it's simply part of the greater pattern of dysfunction in the relationship.

In terms of the message itself, here are some recommendations:

- Keep it simple. A simple declaration might go something like this: "I've been unhappy in our relationship for quite some time now, and have come to realize that I don't want to continue. I've decided I need to part ways with you."

- Don't over-explain. This is not a time to review all of the difficulties in the relationship. That won't serve you or the other person. There is nothing you can say at this point that will bring your partner to enlightenment and transformation. It's you who have become enlightened and are working on transformation — by freeing yourself from this toxic relationship. Anything you say during these kinds of conversations will be used against you, so saying as little as possible and repeating the core message is crucial.

- Avoid blaming the other person. Although you may have come to discover that your love interest is a con artist, and you have been conned, you also made decisions to create the relationship you are exiting. We need to hold people accountable for their behavior, but speaking from a place centered in your own behavior, your own needs, your own desires, and your own decisions will leave you feeling much more empowered and will be less provocative for the other person.

Notice the difference between "You make me unhappy! You cheated on me! You lied to me" and "I've been unhappy and sad and have felt disrespected." While someone might argue by saying "I do respect you," they can't reasonably argue that you don't feel disrespected — your feelings are your feelings. By making your decision about you, rather than about them, you will feel good about what you say and will have a greater chance of keeping the conversation on track.

- Resist the urge to be drawn into a complicated, circuitous interaction about your decision. Your significant other may counter with questions, accusations, threats, promises, requests for more time, requests to meet in person (if you don't live together) to discuss it, etc. Although your desire to be "nice" and "reasonable" and "compassionate" may leave you tempted to negotiate or placate the other person, resist this. Remember that you have thought about this decision carefully. You may have already gone through several break-up/make-up cycles with this person. At this point, return to your message: "I've been unhappy for quite some time and am not going to continue. I've decided I need for us to divorce/break up/part company. I've thought about this carefully and have made my decision. I've said what I need to say, and won't discuss it further, except to take care of the details we need to take care of."

Let's take a closer look at the core issues that are associated with three specific kinds of personality disorders that lead to toxic relationships, and how you might take these into account in communicating the end of a marriage or partnership or other relationship to someone.

Borderline Personality

People with traits of the diagnosis called Borderline Personality Disorder (BPD) struggle with both a fear of abandonment and a fear of intimacy. As a result, their partners often experience a "come here - go away" "push-me/pull-you" "I hate you/don't leave me" dynamic that is confusing and exhausting. People with BPD patterns sometimes have affairs — sexual or emotional — to resolve this dilemma because through affairs they can be connected to someone who is not completely available (e.g., a married person), or they can create distance with someone who is available (their own spouse or partner), and they can play each party against the other, if they choose. People with BPD traits often have short, intense relationships, few enduring friendships, and a great deal of drama in their personal, social, and work lives. They often make impulsive decisions related to sex, food, alcohol, and money, and are prone to tantrums and rages in which they put themselves or others in danger by driving out of control, throwing things, or engaging in violence. Some people with this pattern are prone to threaten suicide, make suicidal gestures, and sometimes carry out suicide attempts. If you are leaving a marriage or relationship with a person who has strong borderline personality traits, you likely will be concerned that the person will harm themselves. We will address this further in the next section of the book, but for now, if this is one or your concerns, chances are that your partner has some borderline traits.

When you break up with a person who has BPD traits, their great anxiety about abandonment is likely to be triggered. None of us likes to feel abandoned, but for a person with BPD, feeling rejected can feel like a life-or-death situation (as it is for all of us when we are babies and toddlers). When a person with these traits feels threatened so deeply, they can make the situation dangerous for themselves and others. It's crucial that you become clear that you are not responsible for anyone else's behavior. Even so, in order to get the best outcome for yourself, it makes sense to be mindful of approaching a breakup with a person with BPD traits in ways that have some chance of reducing their reactivity —and, thereby, your own suffering. Here are some strategies:

- If you have children, you can say to your spouse, "even though this form of our relationship needs to end, we will always be connected through the kids."
- Emphasize that while the relationship needs to change, you have fundamental respect for the other person. "I care about you and about myself, and will continue to. I've made this decision with the hope that it will lead to greater happiness for both of us."
- Acknowledge that ending things isn't easy. "There's much I've loved and enjoyed about you and our time together, but I've come to believe that I will be happier going my own way. I recognize it's hard for you, too, and hope that over time you will find someone with whom you can be happy."

The idea here is to be compassionate but not indulgent, firm but not cruel, and always "on message" that you have made your decision grounded in your needs at this point in your life. By resisting the urge to review all of the difficulties you've experienced in your relationship, and to make them bad and wrong, you take the moral high road, stay grounded in your reality and needs, and reduce to some degree the reactivity with which your partner could respond.

Narcissistic Personality

If the person you're involved with has the traits that define Narcissistic Personality Disorder (NPD), you have probably grown weary of their inflated sense of self-importance, their haughtiness or bragging, their endless need for admiration, and their inability to empathize with you or take your perspective. You may feel a little crazy because people who only know your partner in limited contexts — in work settings, as a Boy Scout leader, or as a competitive athlete — admire their many accomplishments and ways they appear to embody many respectable traits, while in your relationship they operate from entitlement and insecurity.

The narcissist may not see you as a complex human being but as an object to enhance their own image. The narcissist may see you as an object or use you as an audience.

When you leave a narcissist, you're not triggering their sense of abandonment, as with a person who has BPD, but, instead, the narcissist's great ego. How could anyone not want to be with them? The narcissistic person experiences not the pain of losing you in a breakup, but the pain of how losing you diminishes their image. For someone to prefer their own company (or that of someone else) over the companionship of the narcissist creates a narcissistic injury, a puncture wound in the inflated balloon of their ego.

Narcissists have great difficulty handling anything they perceive as criticism, and your ending a relationship will be perceived as a highly critical act. As you probably know from your experience with a narcissistic person, one common response to narcissistic injury is to belittle and berate the messenger. Whereas the narcissist may have at one time built you up emotionally or psychologically because they felt being with you reflected well on them, they may now attempt to degrade you because of your decision to reject a relationship with them.

Specific strategies to use to minimize a narcissist's reactivity and desire for retribution include:

- Acknowledge that the person has many positive qualities and strengths (to the extent that this is true) and focus on the idea that you are not a good match for them; you are freeing them so that they can find their ideal partner.

- The narcissist may say "You can't leave me! I am leaving you first!" in an effort to find some salve for their wounded ego. If this happens, roll with it. The goal, after all, is to separate as quickly and cleanly as possible. If it's easier for the narcissist to believe they are rejecting you, let it work in your favor.

- Emphasize that your decision isn't about their negative qualities but about your need to grow. Pointing out the person's failings, misdeeds, and indiscretions at this point is not productive. It may be tempting to say "I'm leaving you because you are a narcissistic ego-maniac who doesn't give a damn about anybody but yourself," but adding insult to a narcissistic injury will likely make any pushback worse. Simply removing yourself from the situation to the greatest extent possible gives the narcissist the opportunity to figure out for themselves why and how they lost you. Let them do that work, while you do yours.

If your partner is narcissistic, your leaving will likely wound their ego because having a partner — and having you in particular as a partner — represented a status boost for them. If you can accomplish an exit with as little damage to the narcissist's ego as possible, you are less likely to become the target of a protracted power struggle as the narcissist tries to a) win you back; b) make themselves feel better by damaging you or your reputation; or c) attempts to damage you and win you back, simultaneously.

Anti-Social Personality Disorder

There's a lot of overlap between the traits of narcissists and psychopaths (people who meet the criteria for Antisocial Personality Disorder (APD)). A person who is a psychopath often has a grandiose sense of self, an inappropriate sense of entitlement, and an impaired ability to empathize with or be sensitive to the feelings of others --- just like people with Narcissistic Personality Disorder. Psychopaths, however, are known especially for lying and for having a "by any means necessary" approach to achieving their goals. Anything between them and what they desire becomes an obstacle to be eradicated, no matter who is harmed.

When you leave a relationship with a psychopath, you generally don't need to worry about him or her committing suicide, as much as you need to worry about your own safety. When a psychopath experiences an offense to their entitlement, their response often is to punish the offender. For a high functioning psychopath, this might be through psychological torture, attempting to destroy your career or reputation, or playing power games in court over children, property, money, or divorce terms. A lower functioning psychopath may stalk you, harass you, torture people or animals dear to you, or attempt to kill you. From the sociopath's perspective, you "deserve" the "punishment" you're receiving because you offended them or are taking away something that belongs to them (in this case, yourself). Although you are at risk of violence and harassment from people with all kinds of personality disorders, the risk of harm to you is higher with sociopaths because of their general disregard for the law. Again, high functioning sociopaths will know social norms and laws, and will appear to function within these parameters in order to engage in deviant activities without detection. Lower functioning sociopaths are more obvious in their rule violations.

If you know your significant other has served jail time, been convicted of felonies, or received restraining orders in the past, you will need to be especially careful about how you exit. If the person has not been involved with the legal system, but has the traits for which sociopaths are known (lack of empathy, a parasitic lifestyle [you've been supporting them or they have a talent for playing the victim and manipulating others into giving them resources], grandiosity, pleasure in seeing others suffer, retaliation fantasies or behaviors, superficial charm, many fans but few real friends, a focus on "looking good while doing bad"), it's important to handle the exit very carefully.

There is probably much you don't know about this person still, and you may be inclined to underestimate the potential pushback you will experience. Take the Worst Case Scenario exercise very seriously. There's a saying that there are two kinds of sociopaths: those who have been arrested and those who haven't been arrested yet.

Many people involved with psychopaths take the approach of backing out slowly, subtly encouraging the person to lose interest in them, move on to another lover, or initiate the breakup. Others, fearing for their welfare, take radical actions, such as leaving shared households with the possessions they can keep in a car and seeking safety with distant friends or family, or in a shelter, or "vanishing" as best they can from the psychopath's orbit. If you decide that in your situation you will tell the person directly — whether in a conversation or a letter –that you are leaving, here are some tips:

- Become familiar with the strategies for leaving narcissists.
- Avoid having "the conversation" in any location where you are isolated or unable to exit easily.
- Convey that this decision was a very difficult one for you and ask your partner to help you by respecting it.
- As with all breakups, avoid going on the offensive and presenting the other person with a review of the ways they have harmed you. Stay on point: "I've been thinking about this for some time and though it is painful, I've decided I need to be on my own again. I am sad things aren't working out for us."

In a breakup conversation with a psychopath, the goals are to stay on message, keep yourself and anyone else involved safe, and, as much as possible, avoid entering into a power struggle. Expect that everything you say will used against you, so saying as little as possible while repeating the main point as often as necessary is ideal. Remember, psychopaths are con artists; the person may take the news calmly, then ask questions that appear to be caring, such as, "Where will you go?" "Have you talked this over with a therapist?" "Who have you told?" Resist the urge to give up information from your exit plan during this conversation. Knowledge is power, and for a psychopath, power is everything.

IMPROVISATION

Expect a crisis.

You have taken care of your own business. You have battened down the hatches in preparation for the storm. You have envisioned a Worst Case Scenario and mentally rehearsed skillful responses to what you imagine will unfold. You are as prepared as you can be. You have signaled to your Ex, as directly as you can, that you are ending your relationship.

Now, you wait.

Not in the sense of waiting around, doing nothing, holding your breath, of course; more in the sense of being watchful, staying alert, keeping yourself in a position to respond flexibly, adroitly, skillfully. As much work as you have done to get to this moment, what will happen next is unknown. You goal is to avoid falling into reactivity and, instead, to operate like a skillful sailor, adjusting creatively and confidently to the storm you may need to navigate now.

The crisis that comes in response to a breakup, dissolution, or divorce with a toxic person isn't always about how they react to your announcement that you are finished. The crisis can also take place inside of you, as you make your brave stand for a better, happier life for yourself. It can be uncomfortable to face down a bully. It can be uncomfortable to resist begging, seduction, and promises, especially when part of you wants to believe that your person can have a transformation. It can even be uncomfortable when, in response to your declaration of an ending, your Ex responds with silence, giving you the cold shoulder in an attempt to make you uneasy about your decision. It can be uncomfortable to discover spaciousness in the places that your Ex's drama, neediness, or entitled demands used to occupy. It is important to manage the stories in your own head in order to manage any drama that could come your way as your Ex realizes that you are serious about leaving.

Leaving a toxic relationship because you want something better for yourself is a big, bold, courageous move. It's important to see it through. It's important this time to leave for good.

The fourth step in *The Five Step Exit* is Improvisation.

In this section, we'll explore some of the practices that you can use to respond to the "crises" that come up as you make clear you are determined to exit the relationship. Each time you respond to one of these "crises" in a way that affirms your decision, you will become more committed to it. Each time your Ex creates a crisis, you have more confirmation that you have made a healthy decision for yourself. Each time you respond in a skillful way, you will see your situation, yourself, and your Ex a little more clearly, and that will help you move forward.

Responding to the post-breakup or break-up-in-progress crises will test you and your resolve. If you have come this far, I know you can weather the turbulence that could arise now.

Let's make sure you have the strategies you need.

Staying present

You've probably heard about mindfulness training. Maybe you have even gone to a meditation class or a mindfulness-based stress reduction course. If you haven't, when you finish reading this practice, I encourage you to find an on-line resource that will guide you through some simple exercises to help you develop your ability to stay focused in the present, not just during meditation or a class, but in the most challenging moments of your life.

Beyond the wonderful benefits that staying present, following your breath, and cultivating inner tranquility can have for your health and well-being, its practical application to real life troubles becomes readily apparent when you face down ego-wounded narcissists, persons with borderline personality patterns engaging in drama, or psychopaths repositioning themselves to regain power over you.

In the course of your separation from a toxic relationship partner, there may be true crises, moments when someone actually is in harm's way. Staying present in these moments will allow you to respond wisely and skillfully, rather than over-react or become paralyzed. Mostly, however, the "crises" that emerge are not crises at all, but dramas manufactured by your Ex in an effort to distress, confuse, provoke, manipulate, or exhaust you — and to restore their own sense of power and control.

Imagine this: when you first tell the toxic person you are ending the relationship, they seem calm and surprisingly agreeable. A week later, however, the sound of pounding on the front door of your apartment awakens you in the middle of the night. You immediately know who is there. As you get out of bed, the sound of your Ex shouting "Let me in! I know you're there! I know you are cheating on me! If you don't open this door I will know you have been cheating on me all along" confirms what your instincts have already registered: yes, indeed, your Ex is at the door, disturbing the whole neighborhood in the middle of the night. What would be your first response in a situation like this?

Your first instinct may be to open the door to prevent everyone in the vicinity awakening to someone shouting unflattering accusations. Doing that, however, opens you to all kinds of possible risks. If you can stay present and calm in this moment, you will be able to recognize that there are other options, because you can be clear about what's happening:

1. You were sleeping in your own bed, with or without a companion, and you have every right to continue to do so.
2. You have no obligation to open the door.
3. If your Ex awakens the neighbors, it's a reflection on your Ex, not on you.
4. You have no obligation to confirm or deny your Ex's accusations.
5. Your Ex is yelling inflammatory accusations in an attempt to embarrass you enough that you will open the door; the behavior is grossly manipulative.
6. You have no idea what might be awaiting you if you open the door.
7. You cannot predict what will happen if you allow a

distressed, loud, possibly intoxicated Ex into your home in the middle of the night.

8. If you let them in, however, you can predict that you will have rewarded this obnoxious and inappropriate behavior — and put yourself at greater risk of harm (in the form of violence to you or allegations they might make of violence from you, once they are in your home).

9. Most importantly, you have choices:

- Open the door.
- Talk to them through the door; tell them you will call the police if they don't leave immediately.
- Ignore them and go back to bed, hoping they will simmer down.
- Exit your home through a back door or window; go to your car and drive away (while calling the police).
- Stay away from the door, call the police and report the disturbance; wait in an area of the apartment you believe would be safe if your Ex has a gun and starts shooting from where they are. (Think this is preposterous? Remember Pretorius shooting his girlfriend in the bathroom?)
- If you believe your Ex could break into the apartment by pounding on the door, and you cannot slip out some other way, lock yourself, anyone else, and your pets inside your safest room with your phone and something you can use as a weapon, if need be. Wait for the police, who will be able to see the Ex from their exterior vantage point and will be in a better position to assess their dangerousness and diffuse the situation.

By staying present, you will realize that you could open the door, but also that you have no obligation to do so. Your Ex's dramatic appearance at your door does not require you to open it or to address their accusations. At this moment, things are uncomfortable and unpleasant, but nobody risks bleeding to death.

There are some unknowns, however, that could move this from a drama toward a crisis situation. By staying present, you will be more able to reduce the chances that the situation could evolve into something tragic – for example, if your Ex wants to kill themselves in front of you, to come into your apartment and hurt you for "cheating on them," or to destroy your property once inside.

Here are some tools you can use to help yourself stay present, rather than shutting down, being paralyzed, or over-reacting in the difficult situations your Ex may put you in as you put your exit plan into effect:

1. Take a few deep breaths. This helps your nervous system stay calm and you to stay present.

2. Ask yourself, "What is really happening right now?" The answer might be, "Right now, someone is pounding on my door in the middle of the night, yelling obscenities," which allows you to move toward responding to your Ex as you would to anyone pounding on your door, yelling obscenities in the middle of the night. What's happening might be, "I am in a library, reading demands and threats by e-mail on a computer. It's just e-mail, and just a computer. Everything is calm in the library. Sun is coming through the window. There is no crisis here." Asking yourself, "What is really happening right now?" grounds you in the present.

3. Separate what's happening from *your story about what's happening*. If your Ex is trying to harass you by text, recognize that what's happening is that you are having feelings come up because you are reading words on a computer the size of a playing card from someone who is not within striking distance. Your brain's story may be that you need to be fearful in this moment; by focusing on what's really happening —"I'm reading text messages. The world I'm in is no different from how it was 60 seconds ago" — instead of stories or feelings about what's happening, you can stay clearer and more able to respond from a place of centeredness.

4. Pay very close attention to the environment you are in. Note the light, the temperature, the people or trees or traffic around you, the sounds you are hearing, the scents in the air. Noting and focusing on these details can help keep you in the present and aware of what's really happening, rather than getting caught up in the spin that your Ex may be generating.

5. Engage in soothing self-talk that grounds you in the present: "Right now, my Ex is making a nuisance of themselves. This is a hassle for me, and I feel bad for them, but I am safe in this moment and am doing what I can to stop this situation from escalating."

Staying present when drama arrives in the form of threats, unexpected visits, confrontations, stalking, harassing phone calls, or notices of legal actions your Ex might attempt to take against you will allow you to maintain your equilibrium in these trying moments, to respond effectively when a response is necessary (someone is at risk of harm or you are legally required to respond), and to otherwise minimize the drama, fear, or uncertainty your Ex attempts to create as you move forward in your life.

No contact

To go "No Contact" or "NC" is one of the most powerful practices you can use in your effort to end your toxic relationship for good. To go NC means to have no contact with your Ex.

Period.

This advice can be very difficult to hear, and more difficult to enact, especially if you come from a small community or one in which there exist traditions of remaining friendly with Exes, as in LGBTQ communities. Nonetheless, the sooner you can achieve no contact, the more you can accelerate your recovery process. If you share children, you may be unable to achieve NC for some time. The ultimate goal remains "no contact," but you may have to practice "low contact" for a while until that is possible. We discuss that in the next section, but understanding the principles of No Contact will be helpful to you even if you still must interact with your Ex around child custody or child care issues, so read on.

Remember: this is not a general practice for fairly regular relationships that simply don't work out. Many dating relationships, partnerships, and marriages can be amicably resolved in ways that allow both parties to remain on – or eventually return to — cordial terms. No Contact becomes desirable in truly toxic situations because of the many kinds of difficulties that ongoing interactions with a toxic Ex will create in your life.

For some, the toxic relationship may have felt like an addiction. Ending this relationship may look and feel a lot like ending a relationship with alcohol or drugs. You may have tried quitting the relationship previously, only to "fall off the wagon" and return. Addictions change our brain chemistry to keep us coming back for more. When we try to stop using a drug of choice, our brains (and other organs) go through withdrawal, and we can become very, very uncomfortable. The quick fix for this discomfort? A reintroduction of the substance into our system. This gives us some relief — but it undermines our efforts to stop using and requires that we return to square one when we try to end the addiction again. The longer you have no contact with your ex, the more comfortable you will become with being free. When you have a set-back, you undermine your emotional freedom and welfare.

By alternative, you may not feel "addicted" to your partner as much as you feel trapped. You wonder how they will survive without you, because you have come to feel responsible for their health, welfare, well-being, and successes. You know that you are unhappy and that you are not being treated well. You know that you are not thriving and have given up on reaching for your dreams. You may not be addicted to your partner, per se, but addicted instead to a sense of obligation for the person's welfare, or to being a hero or heroine. Going No Contact will give you relief from the responsibility of managing another grown-up's life, and will give your Ex the opportunity to begin to figure out how to take care of themselves. You will be surprised at how well they will do this – even if only by finding someone else to fill your role as their rescuer.

A third possibility is that you have been living in fear for your safety if you end the relationship. You don't feel addicted. You don't see your partner as helplessly dependent. Instead, you believe that when you end the relationship there is a chance that your Ex will become punitive and vengeful — a concern that you must take very seriously. In circumstances like this, you may need to "back slowly away" from the relationship or, by alternative, abruptly end it, depending on the details. In either instance, however, it is especially important that when you are done, you move into No Contact and stay there.

Whether you have been addicted to your person or to rescuing your person or to living in fear of the consequences of exiting, you need to move into the No Contact Zone as soon as you have squared away the details of your dissolution. Ideally, this means simply and completely that you have no contact of any kind for any reason with your Ex.

"No contact" is in some ways a misnomer. It implies that you only need to avoid talking with, e-mailing, texting, or meeting your Ex. As you well know, in the information society we can access information about people without directly interacting with them. More than one of my clients recovering from a toxic relationship with a personality disordered Ex has broken NC when they decided to check out their Ex's Facebook page or website or blog; when this happens, the recovering person always discovers that they have just kicked their own hornet's nest of unpleasant emotions. As a result of exposure to information about their Ex, they experience a setback in establishing their own peace and balance. They also have to deal with the knowledge that trolling their ex's Facebook page for information is intrusive, inappropriate behavior — not far from the behavior of their disordered ex.

No contact means both no contact and no exposure.

Set up your e-mail so that messages from your Ex go to your spam box; un-friend and block them on Facebook, or take yourself off of Facebook altogether; do not answer calls or texts or e-mails from your ex. Indeed, do your best to block them from your phone or get yourself a new number or a new phone.

Tell your committee – your team — that you are going NC and don't want to hear any news or any worries that they have about your Ex, unless they have concerns for your physical safety. If they worry that your Ex is putting someone else in danger, they should call the police, not you. Remember how reinforcement works – your consistency here establishes that this relationship really is over. If you were training a dog to understand that you are not a source of table scraps, it would be important to never, ever, feed the dog from the table. **What you do is far more important than what you say.** If you say you are ending the relationship but continue to engage with your Ex, the behavior says things are not really over. No Contact says you mean business.

There are three goals in No Contact:

The first goal is to end the toxic relationship.

The second is to stop sending the signal to your Ex that their behavior is still relevant, meaningful, disturbing, or noteworthy to you, and thereby to extinguish their attempts to engage you.

The third is to help restore peace to your life, allowing you to "detox" from the relationship and begin the process of recovery by calming your nervous system as peace in your life is restored.

Even when kids and property are not in the picture, there are many issues that initially you will feel require contact —concert tickets, the pets, dividing the housewarming presents, etc. Most of these should have been addressed in your initial thinking about and communication over splitting up. If they were not, consider whether these issues really require contact, or whether your Ex is using them as an excuse to contact you — or vice versa.

Low contact

Not everyone's situation allows for absolute No Contact. If you are approaching a divorce settlement date but have no children, you may need to be in Low Contact until the divorce is final. Most typically, if you are co-parenting children or involved in a custody conflict, absolute NC will be difficult because there will need to be some contact around kid logistics. Still, the less the better, especially because whatever you say could come back to you in court. If your relationship involved children, joint ownership of homes or businesses, or other legal complications, you need to involve legal counsel, if at all possible.

The advantages of having excellent legal advice cannot be overestimated. Having an attorney allows you to limit your contact further, because your attorney will represent you and speak for you. Sometimes, even people who have dated toxic individuals only for a few weeks have had to use counsel to encourage a disordered person to back off when they engage in slander or libel after a relationship ends. If you are working out custody, courts often now use court-monitored electronic messaging systems to allow people to communicate with each other about the details of children's schedules and other issues related to their care. If you must communicate, using these mediums is far better than personal texts or e-mails; they will be observed by the court and your involvement can be kept to communication about logistical details.

If you will co-parent children with a personality disordered Ex, it makes sense to explore the kinds of support children will need to promote their emotional and physical health in the aftermath of your relationship. If you are not a custodial parent and have no legal rights to the children, even if you have been parenting them, prepare for your Ex to use the children as pawns, bargaining chips, or weapons. Do your best to prevent this from happening, even if it means walking away. This can be very difficult, but it models for the children the truth that the right course of action sometimes involves removing yourself from a toxic situation. Children often will seek you out later, when they have the legal right to do so. If you share placement through court order, only communicate with your Ex as briefly as possible about issues that the legal system requires, and do it through legal channels as much as possible. Your Ex may attempt to provoke you into emotional responses by leveling wild accusations at you by text or e-mail or in phone conversations. If you are not mandated to respond, don't.

Document, document, document

As you move into No Contact or Low Contact, and as you experience fallout, it is important that you document what happens.

If your Ex calls, let voicemail answer – not only because of No Contact, but also because voicemail becomes a record. If your Ex comes to your house to confront you and tries to prevent you from leaving by parking their car across your driveway, take a photo of this. If they pound on your door, turn on the video or audio recording function of your cell phone, if you have one, so that their threats are recorded. If you don't have a way to record this but have called the police, ask the dispatcher to stay on the line with you while you wait for police to arrive so that they can hear and witness the yelling.

If you receive threatening texts or e-mail messages, don't reply to them: instead, respond by saving them in documents that you copy in a couple of places (for example, make a Word document that compiles them, print paper copies, and send the messages to a friend by e-mail, which will create a "sent" copy as well as give someone else who cares about you a record of what's happening. Convert text messages to e-mail and/or forward them to a friend).

If your Ex confronts you unexpectedly and leaves you shaken, call someone immediately and report what happened; your memory of the incident may recede if you are emotionally flooded, so ask a friend to write down what you say happened. If it's warranted, call the police to report that you are being harassed. Even if this particular incident doesn't meet the criteria for a legal restraining order that requires your Ex to keep their distance from you, you will begin to build a case in that direction, should you need to seek a restraining order in the future. If your Ex becomes violent with you, go to an Emergency Room and ask that the staff there document your injuries. If your Ex damages your property, take photos before repairing it. Making a police record can be immensely helpful. Even if you live with the person and they are destroying things inside your home, they can be cited.

Always document fallout, whether by keeping whatever your Ex sends to you, photographing it, making a written or recorded description of what has happened, or calling the police so that they make a record. Remember that many people with personality disorders essentially are bullies. Although some are not intimidated by law enforcement, many who intimidate others will back down when they are confronted by law enforcement or a letter from a lawyer that indicates you will take legal action for damages they cause, whether to your property, your person, or your reputation.

The goals of documenting, documenting, documenting are these:

1. Because you may need to take legal action against your Ex, your Ex may take pre-emptive or bogus legal action against you. If you are married or share business ventures or property, or you have children, the legal system will likely be part of your breakup, so having thorough and careful records to support your claims is immensely helpful. It might be hard for anyone to believe that your rich, charming, and good looking Ex physically forced a teenager into the basement and locked her in for the weekend, but if you have video or the distressed messages from the kid, your allegation becomes much more credible.

2. Memory gets messy when we're stressed. Documenting

incidents around the breakup as they happen helps you recall them later.

3. Whether or not the legal system becomes involved with your situation, documenting any pushback, fallout, or drama that unfolds allows you to stay clear about why you want to end your relationship with this person, and will allow you to look back eventually and recognize that yes, it really was this bad.

Recognize what you can and cannot control

You cannot control your Ex.
You cannot control your Ex.
You cannot control your Ex.
You cannot control your Ex.
You can control yourself.

You cannot control what your Ex says about you, what story they tell about you or your relationship, how they misrepresent what happened between you, or how they interact with your relatives or friends. You cannot control what they do at the bank, what they do with the IRS, or whether they lie in court. You cannot control what they say to your kids, whether they make good on the money they owe you, or the amazing speed at which they seem to land a new significant other. None of this is under your control.

The good news, however, is that you can control your own behavior. When the toxic person you're leaving stalks you, you can file for a restraining order. When they vandalize your property, you can call the police. When they misrepresent their finances to the IRS in an effort to evade child support responsibilities, you can ask the IRS to investigate. If they spread lies designed to damage your livelihood, you can sue them for slander or libel. You can do all of these things from a centered place of protecting yourself and anyone else involved.

Everything else, you can let go.

Friends tell you that your Ex is making pointed remarks about having "escaped a paranoid abusive drunk" on Facebook, without mentioning you specifically. You feel your stomach tumble a little bit, especially because you don't drink, do feel victimized and exploited, and have never been paranoid. The information tells you that this is how your Ex will spin you; perhaps it's the same story they told about their last romantic interest, which will also tell you that you have been involved with someone who relates to people as caricatures, someone whose trauma continues to project the same old story onto anyone involved with them. It's useful, interesting, distressing, disappointing information. And you have no control over it. You can only control how you respond, knowing what you know.

As you go through the process of leaving your toxic relationship, there will be much that you cannot control. At first, this may feel scary. Eventually, you may find it liberating to be able to say, "They did what? They said that, eh? Well, that's not under my control. I have nothing to do with that – or with them."

You cannot control your Ex.

You can control yourself.

And that will be enough.

Teamwork

As you were preparing to exit, you put together a team of people who agreed to support you in your efforts to leave your toxic relationship. When blowback/fallout issues emerge, call on your team. They are already aware of your situation and of your effort to liberate yourself from someone who has caused you unnecessary pain and trouble. Indeed, they may have realized before you did that your partner was bad news. If your Ex begins to cause you trouble of one kind or another, these are the people who won't need much of an explanation, won't be surprised by what's happening, and won't hesitate to help you move forward. Keep their numbers at the ready.

As much as you may consider yourself independent and self-sufficient, and as good as you are at solving problems, remember that the mission you've undertaken is not an ordinary break-up that can be managed with a few days on the couch in the fetal position, a few gallons of ice cream, a sports weekend with the guys, a new Match.com profile, or a few heart-to-heart conversations with your BFF's. Ending a relationship with a person who has a narcissistic, antisocial, or borderline personality involves a range of risks and unexpected twists and turns different from the usual course of events in the endings of more healthy relationships. In addition to the professionals you may need on your team — a counselor, an attorney, a financial guide, the police, mental health crisis workers — your friends can provide invaluable clarity, support, and assistance when things get bumpy. Humbling as it may be, don't hesitate to call on the folks you've taken into your confidence if your Ex tries to cause you drama, undermine you further, challenge your decision, or seduce, bully, or manipulate you into reuniting. It often takes a village to support one person ending a toxic relationship.

Responding to accusations and projections

Your Ex needs to have a story explaining why you no longer see them, and the probability that this story will line up with your reality is very, very low. You may hear your Ex's spin directly from them, or you may hear it through the grapevine. No matter its origin, you will likely find their version of reality outrageous, frustrating, bizarre, or worrisome, at first anyway. The day you find it amusing, preposterous, or simply diagnostic, you'll know you're well on your way to recovery.

Often, the story your Ex spins will be a projection. That is, they will accuse you of the behaviors of which they are guilty (this is called "projection") in a story designed to make them look good. For example, a freeloading psychopath might say, "I haven't been able to work because you have been so needy that I have had to take care of you, and now you are kicking me to the curb." It doesn't matter that you have been receiving no "care," or that the three jobs you're working to support the psychopath haven't allowed you to be home to be "cared for." What matters is that you have pulled the plug on their parasitic lifestyle.

So, how do you handle this?

First, recognize that you can't control what your Ex says or the story they tell themselves — although if they spread misinformation in a way that threatens your livelihood, you can sue them.

Second, by paying attention to what your Ex says, you will gain insight on how they operate. Sometimes, this will lead you to new understandings of the strategies they've used to hook you or others in the past, put stories you had taken as true into a new light, and give you some sense of what to continue to expect from them.

Third, if you worry about your reputation as your Ex attempts to destroy or defame you among friends or family, staying honest and non-defensive is usually an effective strategy. If an acquaintance says, "you know, they are pretty convincing, and their version is that you were abusing them (or their child, or their pet) and that's why they left you," it will be challenging for you to hear. If you can stay non-reactive, however, and calmly respond by saying, "Yes—I know they can be believable; that's why it took me so long to get out. I am mortified that the story you heard is their spin on things, and obviously, I can't disprove it. If those things are true, I would advise you to stay away from me, and I understand if you do. All I can ask is that you evaluate me on how I've treated you and how you've seen me behave and who you know me to be."

You may lose some friends in the divorce as your social world changes. This can be sad, but at the end of the process the people who are still in your life are those who see you clearly and value you. As you free yourself from your toxic relationship, you will discover new space in your life for more people, ones you will choose using the wisdom that you have gained from surviving this toxic relationship.

Slow it down

Chances are that you are the hyper-responsible type. Chances are also that you are hyper-responsive. You are the sort of person who feels compelled to answer e-mails, return phone calls, and honor as many requests as you can from friends, family members, co-workers, and the stranger down the street. Unfortunately, in your relationship with a toxic person, your responsibility and responsiveness have also been used against you. The toxic person in your life has come to expect that you will always reply, and will do so on their timeline.

Part of the fallout you experience will include a range of efforts to re-engage you. Some of these may be friendly overtures. Others of these will be pointless, trivial questions. You may receive dramatic or crazy-sounding messages that threaten you or that beg for your help. What are the goals of your toxic Ex in these efforts?

1. To establish that you will still respond to them.

2. To establish that you will respond to them on their timeline.
3. To collect information from you as you respond to them.
4. To throw you off — either by lulling you into complacency (if they are being friendly) while they prepare for some kind of emotional ambush so that they receive confirmation that they still can manipulate you to achieve their own goals.

In most instances, you will benefit greatly from making a conscious commitment to slowing things down. In most instances, it will not be necessary for you to respond directly to your disordered Ex. If they hassle or threaten you, call the police.

In one instance, a disordered woman sent threatening messages in an effort to re-gain access to her former partner's home. "I will bring the police" and "The police are aware" and "I am at the police station! It is illegal for you to prevent me from coming in" were among the statements she sent via text and e-mail, demanding that her former partner return home and let her in, under police escort.

Wisely, the former partner noted that if the police were indeed interested in giving the sociopath access to the home, it would be police officers making contact, not the Ex. She ignored the demanding texts and e-mails, called the police herself, and showed the messages she'd been receiving to the officers who arrived. "That lady has some mental health issues, doesn't she?" the officers noted, after reading the demanding messages threatening to "Bring the police" and "Ruin your reputation." Subsequently, they contacted the irate Ex and warned her to stop the messaging or risk harassment charges. The harassment campaign stopped, and the harassed former partner wasn't required to let the Ex into her home or deal with her directly again.

It can be hard to slow things down. By practicing mindful presence, recognizing that you are no longer accountable to your Ex (except in instances in which the courts have mandated contact) and reminding yourself that you are on your own timeline, you will get better at it. If you have acquired a new phone number for everyone else in your life and directed your Ex's e-mail into your spam folder, you are doing yourself a favor in this direction.

I can think of two exceptions:

1. There is an imminent danger to yourself or someone else in your immediate vicinity
2. There is a direct threat of homicide, other bodily harm, or suicide beyond your immediate reach

In both of these instances, you will need to respond quickly. Nonetheless, your response must not come from a place of panic, but from a clear-headed, centeredness that allows you to take quick action to reduce both harm and drama.

What to do when your Ex contacts you: A review

Let's assume that sooner or later, your Ex will contact you.

Let's review what you will do.

First, do not respond right away; that would signal that you remain attentive, whether through fear, obligation, guilt, or misplaced hope that your Ex has now experienced enlightenment.

Ignore casual "Hey, how are you" or "I miss you" texts or other messages that have no meaningful content...if they happen to make it through the filters you should have constructed by now. These messages are simply your Ex's way of saying, "Testing, testing: are you still hooked in?" "Do I still pull your strings?" "Do you still want me?" "Can I still rile you up?"

If a message is "about" something, such as a date you had planned that won't happen now, decide if the issue has any real impact on the big picture of your life. If it doesn't, don't respond. Again, these kinds of messages are not about what they seem to be about, but, instead, are efforts to engage you.

If your Ex contacts you to berate you, fight with you, threaten you, belittle you or, by alternative, to flatter your ego, do not respond. Save these messages, however, because you may need them at some point for legal matters.

If your partner contacts you about some crucial unresolved business, respond as minimally as possible. Your Ex's sense of urgency no longer dictates your reality. Give yourself breathing room to consider if, how, and when you want to respond. "I got your message" is a great phrase to use if you feel you need to say something, such as when you are still in contact because you are in the limbo between the break up and the official divorce decree. If the person becomes demanding or bullying by phone, text, e-mail, or social media do not respond directly. If the content of their messages is threatening or harassing, or makes you concerned that they might hurt themselves, contact police and your lawyer; they can deal with your Ex directly and effectively. Do not inconvenience yourself in the face of their demands; you have done that for too long.

If it is absolutely necessary to your own welfare to respond, do give yourself plenty of room to contemplate how to address your Ex. Go to a friend or therapist to design the most effective and limited way to do so. *You nearly always benefit by slowing things down under these circumstances. If nobody is bleeding, it is not an emergency.*

If your Ex threatens suicide, call the police and report the threat; let them respond as they are trained to do.

Never respond directly to harassment by your ex unless you are at immediate risk of physical harm. And if you are being harassed, call the police. In sum: make a commitment to have two feet in the no contact zone; do not accept information about your ex from friends unless it pertains to your safety or welfare; do not creep their Facebook page or lurk around their website or blog; do not stretch beyond the boundaries of the No Contact Zone unless truly necessary, and then communicate in ways that are clear and as little reinforcing as possible. If you are tempted to say something obnoxious, stop yourself. Imagine whatever you write being read aloud in court or appearing in a local paper. If it doesn't pass the "how would I feel if everyone I know sees this" test, don't write it.

Suicide threats

Many partners leaving people with personality disorders face the possibility that their Ex will kill themselves. Sometimes, they have this concern because the person has a history of suicide attempts. Sometimes, they have this concern because there is a long history of suicide threats and gestures, even if there is no history of attempts. Because nobody wants to feel responsible for someone killing themselves, suicide threats become a profoundly powerful potential weapon of manipulation.

Here, I'm going to give you a little crash course in suicidality as it relates to people with personality disorders. Depression sometimes leads to death by suicide, too, and needs to be considered a bit differently from how we consider suicidality connected to personality disorders - the focus of what I'm sharing here.

It will be helpful for you to have some terms that will allow you to think as clearly as possible about any suicidal behavior — words or actions — that comes up as you move closer and closer to accomplishing absolute No Contact.

Here are some key concepts:

We can think of suicidal behavior along a continuum, from suicidal thinking, to threats, to suicide gestures, to suicide attempts. Statements a person makes to others indicating that they will kill themselves fall into the category of "threats" — threats are different from the expression of suicidal thinking that people with depression often report to their loved ones. Many people with personality disorders make **suicide threats** without following through on them because their true intention is not to kill themselves but, instead, to manipulate other people into paying attention, staying with them, giving them money, etc. **Suicide gestures** are behaviors that are not highly lethal but that people use to back up their threats. For example, a person could say they parked their car next to a lake, contemplating driving in. They could cut their bodies (sometimes this is not suicidal behavior at all) but stop themselves from cutting so deeply that they will die from blood loss. In a **suicide attempt**, a person takes action to kill themselves. Suicide attempts can be sorted into "high rescue" and "low rescue" attempts. A person who swallows a bottle of pills in front of their partner is making a high-rescue attempt. A person who takes a bottle of sedatives then goes out on a night when the temperature is below freezing and lies down on an icy pond in a deeply wooded area is making a low-rescue attempt.

I offer you this information because the risk of suicide by a person who has BPD traits and is feeling abandoned is very real, just as the risk of you being manipulated by suicide threats and gestures by someone who has no desire to kill themselves is also very high.

So the question is this: how will you know the difference?

Here's the answer: you won't.

You may have hunches or guesses, and you may be able to predict what your Ex will do based on their previous behavior, but in any particular situation, you will be unable to determine whether your Ex is engaged in manipulation or in an actual suicide attempt – or in both simultaneously.

Your best strategy for responding, then, is to plan to call the police to have them assess the person's risk every time suicide is on the table. If your Ex is prone to sending texts saying, "If I kill myself, it's your fault," (and you are still reading their texts!), the best response is to call the police and report it, rather than texting the person back, calling them, going out to find them, or otherwise engaging with them. You are responding and doing what's appropriate by calling the police, and you are taking yourself out of the drama by turning it over to professionals. If the threat is real, the person is in the right place. If the threat is an effort to get your attention, the person will see that they no longer have direct access to you, but will have the attention of police and social workers.

Threats to destroy you

Unfortunately, if your toxic Ex is more narcissistic or anti-social (psychopathic) than borderline, you may be on the receiving end of threats to your well-being rather than suicide threats to theirs.

We know that when people leave relationships characterized by intimate partner violence (also called "domestic violence" though this also happens in relationships that don't involve cohabiting), they are most at risk of being killed as they are leaving. Even though they have been on the receiving end of violence in the relationship for some time, it is when the victimized person indicates that they are leaving for good that their life is most in danger. Many times, batterers would rather kill their partners than accept that the partner be happy without them or with someone else.

Clearly, the dynamics of battering relationships and abusive relationships with people with personality disorders overlap significantly. From my perspective, battering relationships reflect the behavior of personality-disordered toxic partners. Even if no physical violence has taken place, the power and control issues, the mixed messages, and the break-up/make up cycles are all essentially the same. If your Ex's personality pattern is consistent with that of Narcissistic or Anti-social Personality Disorder, or there's any indication that your Borderline Ex has ever been violent with anyone (you, Ex's, children, pets, property), the fallout of ending the relationship may very well include threats to your welfare.

Sometimes the threats and behaviors will be in the form of physical aggression. Sometimes, however, narcissists and psychopaths will carefully avoid direct physical threats to your safety and instead focus on something else important or dear to you, such as your professional reputation or your status in your neighborhood.

What can you do if this comes up?

First, if you are leaving a domestic relationship in which there has been physical violence, minimize the risks of direct contact with your Ex as much as possible. If you are in a situation in which you need to have ongoing contact with the Ex and you have the legal right to enter your shared home — for example, you need to go back to retrieve belongings that you can't live without — you can ask for police presence to ensure everyone's safety.

Second, if you are having a direct encounter with your Ex, minimize your time in their physical presence. Don't go anywhere in a car with them, and limit your contact to public venues. Don't stay late at a restaurant so that your cars are the only ones in the parking lot. If you are leaving work and your Ex appears in the vicinity without prior arrangement, return to your workplace, call police, and wait there until they come. Every year, many people are shot in parking lots by former partners.

Always trust your own instincts and judgment. Remember that narcissists and sociopaths are bullies. They enjoy watching you sweat. In many instances, showing no fear pays off. In other situations, however, submission and pretending to agree with the abuser's agenda has saved lives. If you have moments like these in the Improvisation phase, trust your own intuition, in the form of that small clear voice inside you, to guide your actions.

If your Ex isn't threatening your physical welfare but is "blowing up your phone," making demands of you and suggesting that "there will be consequences" if you don't comply, you have a few options. One is simply to ignore this until they become tired of being ignored.

If things are squared away enough that you can enact No Contact, please do. If you know your Ex is lighting up your phone with crazy messages, you don't have to read them. You can ask a friend to review them every couple of days for you and let you know if there's anything meaningful happening. Remember, you are living your life on your timeline, and aren't going to waste another precious hour on this character, if you have a choice.

If the threats become harassment, even via email or text, you can ask the police for assistance. Sometimes a narcissist who is threatening to have the police come after you can be very surprised and thrown off of their game when they themselves are contacted by the police and told to stop. Not only does this say to the narcissist that you are no longer playing the game on their terms and that they themselves must consider what they are willing to risk; tt also surprises them that you are no longer willing to be a good victim. This may help them move along more quickly to someone like you used to be — someone of whom they can easily take advantage.

Unplug the Hoover

Sometimes the blowback from leaving a toxic relationship takes the form of unpleasant, obnoxious, and frightening behaviors. At other times, you may be the target of "love bombing" similar to that you received at the beginning of this relationship. The person you are leaving may suddenly appear to become your dream mate, your ideal lover, the most affectionate and sexually exciting partner you could imagine.

Don't fall for it.

I learned the term "Hoovering" from the folks who manage an online support network for partners of people with Borderline Personality Disorder. "Hoover" is the brand name of a vacuum cleaner, and "Hoovering" refers to the compelling sucking force of the machine. Survivors casually refer to a toxic partner's efforts to re-engage someone who is in the process of leaving as "Hoovering." If you can get some distance from your relationship, you will begin to see your toxic Ex's Hoovering strategies for what they are: manipulations.

If you have been in an on-again off-again relationship, you have been through a round or two of hoovering already. Your partner may have dumped you, and you may have been relieved for the opportunity to move on....only to have them reappear a few days or weeks later full of affection and enthusiasm and behaving as though nothing had happened. If you are familiar with the famous three-stage cycle of domestic violence, you will recognize the pattern: first comes the tension-building phase; then comes the explosive incident; and then the make-up/honeymoon phase.

The honeymoon phase of an abusive relationship usually involves a lot of Hoovering.

What makes you vulnerable to being sucked back in this way?

Even when you have decided to leave, to get out for good, after a long, hard look at all of the factors in your relationship, there remains part of you that wants to be incorrect, part of you that wants to discover that you were not conned, that your love was warranted after all, that your time was not wasted, and that your Ex has finally had an epiphany about how they need to change to have your love. Part of you wants to believe that you can still find happily-ever-after with this person. When your Ex begins to try to Hoover you, they tap into the part of you that still can't and won't and doesn't want to believe that they are who they are.

Like that little fix of an addictive substance that provides some temporary relief from withdrawal, suspending reality and allowing yourself to be sucked in by a Hoover Maneuver can feel nice —for a day or two. Soon, however, it becomes clear that you have given up your power and are suffering again as you have been suffering all along.

So: what to do?

First, be on alert for Hoover Maneuvers. These come in a variety of forms, from the apparently meaningless "Hey, I miss you" text to full out Big Romantic Gestures, to promises of reform. You probably know already your toxic person's approach, so be attuned to signs of "the same old story." On the other hand, if your Ex uses a new strategy at this point because they realize you are more serious than ever before, you might be vulnerable to believing they finally have "gotten it." Be alert for innovative Hoover Maneuvers, as well as variations on the usual theme.

If you are in No or Low Contact, you will recognize that these overtures require no response. If you are truly in No Contact, you won't be seeing their messages! Yes, it seems nice that they have texted an apology, but it's too late, and you don't need to respond, no matter how it violates your sense of good manners to ignore them. (Besides, mature adults don't carry out their emotional business by text.) The same is true if you are moving toward No Contact, slowly peeling away but still being exposed to their behavior. Silence is powerful. You have indicated that you are finished with the relationship. You have nothing more to say.

What if you get Hoovered, and you fall hook, line, and sinker for one of your Ex's ploys to suck you in? Ah, well. It happens to most of us. When you recognize that you have been Hoovered again, name it and back away as quickly as possible. Become conscious of the strategy your Ex used to provoke you into breaking Low or No Contact, so that you can recognize your vulnerability to this approach and be more savvy about how your Ex operates. Being in full No Contact or minimalist Low Contact often doesn't happen overnight, and many of us find ourselves Hoovered once or twice along the way. Most people with addictions who move into recovery have setbacks now and again. This doesn't mean all is lost, just that one's coping mechanisms became overwhelmed. In your case, you are detoxing from someone poisonous to you. When you are imperfect at it or have a setback, forgive yourself, laugh if you can, and then get back on the wagon.

Cardinal focus

Depending on the shape your Ex's pushback takes, there may be times when you doubt yourself. If your Ex attempts to Hoover you with the magical words you wish to hear, you may feel like Ulysses hearing the song of the sirens — you will know that you would be better off not hearing them at all (as in no contact!), but because you are hearing them, know that you need to ask your crew members to tie you to the mast of your ship to avoid running it aground.

What can you do when you experience the torturous temptation of your Ex's illusionary promises?

Remember the list of painful incidents that you made when you worked your way through the Snake Naming exercise of *The Five Step Exit*? Find that list and review it. Of all the distressing things that your Ex has done, which is the most disturbing to you? Choose that event from the list. We'll call this a Cardinal Event.

Recall the Cardinal Event in as much detail as possible. Remember what was happening prior to it and where it started to turn nightmarish or appalling. What exactly did your Ex do? What regard did your Ex show for your welfare or feelings during this incident? How did you feel at the end? What was the worst part of the incident? How would you feel if someone behaved this way toward the person you love most in the world? Would you advise them to continue in the relationship or to reunite with the other person after a breakup?

Any time you are tempted to reconnect with your Ex, go back to this negative Cardinal Event, remembering what it taught you about your Ex's character and what kinds of treatment you can expect from them. No matter what they may be saying, their behavior toward you tells the truth about what you can expect in the future.

When kids are used as weapons

If you believe your children are being abused in the care of their personality disordered parent, report this to child welfare authorities or police, and teach the kids how to take care of themselves physically and emotionally when they are away from you.

Do not be surprised if your personality disordered Ex creates very tricky situations for you with your children. There will be times when you will be in a no-win situation, especially if your Ex's abuse or neglect of your children is not well-documented and the court has ordered visitation with them. The children may resist visitation or undermine it in various ways, resulting in your feeling forced by the courts to deliver your kids to their abusive other parent or risk losing your own custody of them. Each family's scenario is different, shaped by the style of local courts, the lawyers involved, how your Ex's pathology expresses itself, the age of the kids, etc.

While each person navigates this complex dynamic differently, it is important in all cases to know what your priorities are, to provide your children with consistent, solid parenting when they are with you, and to pursue through whatever means available to you strategies to limit contact with your disordered Ex if their abuse or neglect of the children rises to levels of concern that the courts would recognize. Document, document, document, while shoring your children up as best you can.

If you lose access to the children because you had no legal rights in them, do your best to let the kids know that your exit is not about them, and that when they are of age, you will be happy for them to find you.

Thought eviction

So, you are totally committed to ending your toxic relationship, reclaiming yourself, and having the best damned life possible.

And yet.

You find yourself occupied and pre-occupied by ruminations about your Ex. You wonder if they really were as bad as you think they are. You wonder if they know how much hurt they cause — whether they do what they do on purpose, or do what they do mindlessly. You wonder what went wrong in their childhood. You wonder how they looked as attractive as they did at the beginning. You wonder if other people are hip to them. You wonder if they ever can get better, if they ever can be fixed.

And you wonder why you can't stop wondering.

I encourage you to ask a different question: "How?"

There are many reasons that victimized partners remained preoccupied (maybe even obsessed) with questions focused on their narcissistic, borderline, or anti-social Ex. At this point, those reasons aren't nearly as important as learning some strategies for stopping this practice, this mental habit. Here's my recommendation:

First, accept that this focus on your Ex and their history and future is mostly an artifact of their manipulation of you in your relationship with them.

Second, acknowledge that you can make choices about what you concentrate on.

Third, notice that when you are focusing on your toxic Ex you are not focusing on your own dreams, plans, work, or welfare.

Fourth, make a commitment to focus on your own dreams, plans, work, and welfare rather than on a person you cannot change with a story you will never fully understand. Consider this re-direction an investment in yourself.

Fifth, when you notice your mind returning to the well-worn groove of pre-occupation with your Ex, gently bring your thoughts back to focusing on something that will serve you better: your own dreams, plans, work, or welfare.

As you work with your thoughts in this way, you will be less and less preoccupied with questions about your Ex and more and more engaged with questions that improve your life.

RECOVERY

Your recovery can begin now, even if you are still in the throes of a painful relationship. The sooner you consciously begin to adopt practices designed to promote your own well-being and happiness, the easier it will be for you to finish any unfinished business in your toxic relationship and to move into the next phase of your life, one that can be infused with happiness and joy. So, whether you read this section while you are still contemplating an exit or arrive here when you are free but still tending a broken heart, I hope you will begin to adopt some of these practices now. Some are daily practices; some are rituals that you might undertake once. All are designed to help you re-ground yourself in your own life, desires, and wellbeing, and to help bring you in touch with other modes of self-care that may be especially and uniquely helpful to you.

Recovery is the fifth step in *The Five Step Exit*.

The main principles for recovery center on exquisite self-care (I'll also call this ESC). People who have been in toxic relationships often become un-centered and alienated from their own needs and desires as they focus on the needs and dramas of demanding partners. They often come to fear expressing their own needs and wishes in response to a partner's narcissism, criticism, or cruelty. As you orient yourself toward recovery, you will become increasingly re-grounded in your own needs and desires and able to experience the ease and happiness that are yours to enjoy.

What are you recovering? By beginning to cultivate exquisite self-care for your physical body, your energetic, emotional, and spiritual self, your sexual self, and your social life, you are recovering peace, self-direction, ease, health, delight, and joy. You are recovering access to small pleasures, large dreams, and social stability. You are, in essence, healing yourself and your life and, in so doing, helping also to heal the world.

Exquisite self care: ESC =TLC

In an earlier exercise, I asked you to identify a person or other spirit that you trust to want the best for you, and to call this person up in your mind when you have questions about whether you're being treated well. We practiced asking how your Constant (as the writer Jackson Mackenzie, author of *Narcissist Free* (2015), brilliantly calls this person) would respond if they were watching the scene you're in. I asked you to use this as a kind of litmus test for whether the behavior you're encountering is okay, if you have doubts. If your Constant wouldn't be happy to see you treated this way, or if you wouldn't be happy to see your Constant treated this way, you have your answer.

As you move deeper into your recovery from a toxic relationship, you can use your sense of your beloved Constant in a different way – to help you retrain yourself to give yourself exquisite self care, ESC. If you are like most survivors of toxic relationships, you have given away much in terms of your resources of time, energy, creativity, and money, and your toxic partner has benefitted while you have left yourself in a situation of depletion and suffering. As you recover, I encourage you to adopt this goal: learning to value yourself deeply enough and treat yourself with such exquisite care that you restore your physical, emotional, and financial wellness. You need to become your own best friend.

This could be a tall order at the moment, given that you may be feeling desperate about just keeping your life functioning at a minimum. You may be moving in with relatives, relocating, looking for a job, and worried about legal concerns related to separation or divorce. "Who has time for exquisite self-care while all of this is going on?" you ask. My response is this: when have you needed it more?

I wish I had a survivors' fund from which I could write six-month grants to give folks a brief time-out full of massages and down-time and good organic food, play dates with puppies and kittens, great sex with sane, kind, partners, outdoor adventures, music and dance and chanting and travel. Heavens knows, you've earned it. I can't yet offer an Exquisite Self Care Recovery Grant, but I am confident that you can grant yourself exquisite self-care, even in the midst of the difficulties your toxic relationship leaves in its wake.

How?

One breath at a time.

The first piece of ESC involves getting in touch with what it looks like and how it feels. For many of us, we're in touch with the giving side of this more than the receiving. Recall a time when you offered exquisite care and kindness to someone you really, unequivocally love/d. Perhaps it was putting a warm cloth on the forehead of an ill grandparent, or soothing an animal in distress. Maybe it was comforting a child who needed a hug. Call up inside yourself how it felt to see this beloved spirit and to offer them the best kindness and care and comfort you could muster in the moment, even if that was "only" speaking in soothing, reassuring tones.

Now, imagine giving yourself this same quality of kindness, care, and presence.

Hold yourself accountable to creating this kind of kindness, care, and presence for yourself. If you are feeling depleted: trust that you can engage in many of the ESC practices here in small doses, without much money, and in brief periods of time ("getting more sleep" being an exception). If you want to add an element of fun challenge, commit to increasing your ESC while staying within these two parameters:

Keep the financial expense to under $5

Keep the time involved to 30 minutes or less

Many of the best things in life are free: lying on your back watching clouds or stars, standing on a beach with your feet in the sand, listening to the water caress the shore, taking a hot bath (a luxury in many places), taking the time to enjoy a peach or a hot cup of tea, listening to music, dancing in your living space, sitting or walking with a friend, resting. This section of the book offers many specific self-care practices for you to use as you recover or reinvent your life, rediscover your spirit, and reclaim your sense of self. The practices here represent only a few of the ways you might expand your ESC plan at present. I have chosen many that you might think of as "transformation on the cheap." The most important element in recovery, the principle at its heart, is to have an evolving commitment to Exquisite Self Care.

Accepting your grief

One of the differences between splitting up with a healthy person and one with a toxic personality is the degree to which your feelings about the break-up are complicated. In a dissolution process, you are likely to experience a range of feelings — sadness, hurt, anger, relief, grief, regret — no matter who is initiating the ending. In ending relationships with personality disordered people, these feelings still come up, but they are often accompanied by complicating feelings of confusion and self-judgment. People in your situation often ask "Why do I feel so bad about this break-up when they treated me so badly?" People ask why they continue to focus their thoughts and feelings on a person who exploited them or lied to them or cheated on them, and why they can't just feel relief and move on. The normal feelings associated with relationships ending are intensified by the craziness of the relationship; in addition, they are complicated by self-judgment about having these feelings at all because the feelings seem "illogical" in light of the evidence.

What do you need to know if you are going through this right now?

First, recognize that the question, "Why do I keep focusing on this when it was so toxic?" is totally normal. Accept that it is more common than not to have this experience as part of the process of your recovery. As you do your work and begin to create the next phase of your life, these questions will fade.

Second, understand that even though your Ex's difficulties deceptions, and exploitation undermined your relationship, the relationship still held importance for you. No doubt you invested much energy, time, caring, and good will in an effort to cultivate it and make it succeed. It's sad when relationships don't work out, and we grieve when they are over. As with any other relationship you cared about, it's okay to go through a grief process now – even though what you are grieving is a) your image of the relationship; b) your hopes for yourself in the context of the relationship; and c) the parts of yourself that were exploited or rejected in the relationship.

Third, when exploitation and deception took place, you didn't know that, initially — you dutifully went about the business of making the relationship work. In fact, you probably worked over-time to have the relationship, while feeling sorry for your partner — who was playing you all the while. You gave the relationship much and received little in return, ultimately. As the truth of your partner's behavior surfaced, it became difficult to reconcile with your idealized perception of them, and with the ways they have worked to deceive you through love-bombing, reassurance, denial, grand gestures, and "Hoovering." Unlike losing to death a dear partner who treated you well, the complicated nature of your relationship creates a complicated grief process, such as when an abusive or absent parent dies. Although the survivor may grieve, what they grieve is not the loss of their connection with the parent, but the loss of the possibility of having a parent with whom they could connect or who cared for them.

So, how can you navigate through this complicated, complex grief?

1. Don't resist it. Accept that you will grieve the relationship, no matter how "illogical" that may seem or how much pressure you may feel from friends and family to "not spend one minute more" thinking about the relationship. The fastest way to that destination is accepting and experiencing the grief, rather than ignoring, denying, and suppressing it.

2. As quickly as possible, remove all unnecessary triggers of grief from your surroundings.

3. Devote some time to sinking down into the grief and becoming clearer about what you are grieving. This may be "I am grieving how I felt to see myself as a generous, loving partner" or "I am grieving the loss of the possible future life we had talked about" or "I am grieving my image of my former partner, which did not line up with the reality of who they are." The clearer and more specific you can become about what you are grieving, the easier it will be for you to loosen up the grief and let it move through you.

4. Create a "freedom ritual" — you'll see some ideas about this elsewhere in this section — to formalize your grief and create

an opportunity for closure.

5. Practice gratitude. Along with the grief, experience gratitude that you can feel grief, that you register loss, and that relationships are meaningful to you — this is not the case for everyone, and is likely not the case for your toxic Ex. Continue to extract value from your relationship by recognizing what you have learned from it; continue to learn from it about yourself, about the world, and about the kind of relationships you want to cultivate.

Over the course of time, as you accept the ending of the relationship and your grief about it, and move increasingly into a place of gratitude for its lessons, the grief will lighten up and you will be able to focus your attention more and more on the present and the future.

Sleep

Many people who have experienced toxic relationships find that their sleep has become disrupted, disordered, or problematic. Sometimes, toxic partners use sleep deprivation to keep you unbalanced by staging late night screaming matches or waking you up to engage you in some sort of drama. Sometimes, partners who have developed a pattern of codependency worry excessively about the toxic person's welfare. Perhaps they stay out late drinking or work into the wee hours to make up for irresponsibility at their jobs, then travel deserted roads in the dark after telling you how unsafe the driving conditions are. Some toxic partners make suicide threats. You may be exhausted and sleep-deprived because a disordered partner has been leaning on you financially and, unable to maintain your boundaries, you have been over-working to keep their financial house —and yours –in order. Clearly, sleep deprivation has many possible roots in toxic relationships, and if you are suffering from it, I encourage you to make it a high priority issue on your recovery list.

Good and plentiful sleep helps us in many ways: it allows our bodies to better regulate our hormones; it allows our brains to process information in ways that differ from when we are awake; it often helps us regenerate our creativity; and it helps us to stay emotionally grounded and, as a result, to see situations more clearly, make better decisions, and feel more at ease.

The research on sleep offers sometimes contradictory recommendations about optimal sleep time and patterns. Although some clinicians recommend eight hours of continuous sleep as the standard for adults, some recent research suggests that a couple of three or four hour stretches of good sleep interspersed with periods of wakefulness for sex or meditation or other activities is just as restorative. Certainly, you know whether you are exhausted. You probably know what your normal/healthy sleep rhythm and cycles are; if these have become disrupted, their restoration is very important.

There are various strategies for resetting your sleep clock. For some people, the short-term use of sleep medication—even for a few nights—can be remarkably helpful. More holistic approaches include attending to "sleep hygiene." This includes making sure the room in which you sleep is cool and dark and not a place where you spend a lot of time working, using technology, or watching television, if at all possible. Making a commitment to regular or semi-regular sleep and wake times can also be valuable. Showering or bathing before bed, which allows your body temperature to drop and promotes sleepiness, can be helpful, as can drinking a number of teas that promote sleep and relaxation (any health food store or holistic pharmacy can recommend these). Scheduling body work or energy work at times that allow you to sleep afterward can also be beneficial. Spending an hour winding down in low-demand, low technology, low light activity before you go to bed also helps. When people spend an hour before bed easing their way into rest, they often discover they are far more tired than they realized, which also helps sleep to come.

Consistent with "no contact," constructing a sleep practice that makes it impossible for your toxic former partner to interrupt your sleep is crucial. If you find yourself checking Facebook or text messages or e-mail to see if your Ex has tried to contact you, practice self-discipline in whichever ways are necessary to prevent yourself from this form of self-abuse. Again, if you need to get a new phone number, do so.

If, after using various self-care practices, you discover that your sleep is still problematic, seek professional help from a clinician who specializes in sleep disorders. She or he can work with you on a plan to structure a conscious period of sleep deprivation that, paradoxically, can allow you to reset your sleep clock and cultivate more extended periods of deep and restorative sleep.

May your dreams become sweet again.

Eat. Good. Food.

It may surprise you that I am spelling this out, but if your situation has been dire and stressful and you have been feeling strained and out of sorts and depressed, you may need to be reminded that Eating Good Food is a vital part of any ESC plan.

And when I say Good Food, I don't mean ice cream. Even if it's organic.

I know: it may have been justifiable to give yourself a meltdown weekend in which you lay on the couch, watched trashy TV, and ate a couple of gallons of ice cream. But that time has passed, and it's time to become oriented toward exquisite self-care in the form of food.

You may experience various kinds of resistance coming up when you read this, objecting that you don't have time to cook, can't afford to eat out, and need to survive on dollar meals from McDonalds because the toxic Ex has left you financially strapped and you are driving from job to job working 90 hours a week and putting out various financial fires. I'm going to ask you to reconsider, for the following reasons:

1. *End game, baby:* Living on junk food can only get you so far, so long. At some point, especially if you are going to continue to face fallout and pushback, stress and crappy nutrition will catch up with you in the form of an illness that will make your situation even worse. In order to persevere through what's happening, your ESC needs to include food.

2. *Mental health*: More and more evidence confirms what you already know: food high in sugar or high in starches that are converted to sugar in the body and disturb your intestinal ecology feed depression and other emotional difficulties. Increasing evidence supports the theory that our emotions are connected to our intestinal tract — our "gut feelings" are quite literally in our guts — and to have a healthy intestinal tract you need to consume very little in the way of sugar, lots of whole foods, and fermented products like sauerkraut,

pickles, kimchee, kefir, and yogurt, and/or add probiotic supplements to your diet. In addition to feeling better emotionally, your stamina and optimism will improve, and you may lose some weight, if you carry excess, by learning how to feed your gut in healthy ways.

3. *The practice of self-kindness and care:* By feeding yourself well —yes, foods that are organic, healthy, and varied— you practice lovingkindness with yourself and begin to reinforce standards for how you wish to be treated by others. As you have more experience treating yourself in caring ways, you will be better able to screen out people in your social world who don't treat you at least as well.

4. *Money in your freedom fund:* Take a little extra time to plan meals ahead that focus on inexpensive whole food ingredients and maximize vegetables, and you will discover yourself feeling better and richer.

Go outside and play

If your life doesn't include significant time outside, I urge you to add time outdoors to part of your exquisite self care plan. One of the most valuable resources for your health and wellbeing is just a few steps beyond the exit sign, in the great outdoors.

Outside time offers many benefits to you, including:

1. *Exposure to natural light:* If you allow the sun to kiss your skin, your stores of Vitamin D, made by the human body when exposed to sun, increase. Vitamin D is crucial for the healthy functioning of your immune system. Scientists believe Vitamin D also makes positive contributions to our mental health, cognitive functioning, and ability to ward off a range of diseases. Yes, you could take a supplement —and perhaps should—but why not allow your body to do what it is designed to do, at no expense to you?

2. *Direct contact with the planet:* If you take off your shoes and walk on grass, ground, rock, or sand, your body benefits from having direct contact with Earth, which has its own electrical charge. Current research suggests that the benefits of walking barefoot outside include better immune function,

glucose control, and sleep, reduced pain and blood viscosity (significant in heart attack risk), and changes in the brain indicating greater ability to handle stress.

3. *Greater integration with the local environment*: Some fascinating research suggests a complex and beautiful relationship between our bodies' exposure to local soils, eating food grown in our local environments, and our immune systems. If your time outside includes getting your hands in the dirt, all the better for your immune system and your sense of connection, both of which have no doubt been disrupted by your toxic relationship.

4. *Greater understanding of how we are connected*: Many cultures have recognized the healing benefits of spending time in nature and, in particular, of spending time in forests. The Japanese have recently conceptualized the practice of spending healing time in the woods as "Shinrin-Yoku" or "forest bathing." Empirical research supports the idea that forest bathing has these benefits: increased immune system functioning, ability to focus, energy levels, ability to recover from illness and surgery, ability to sleep well, and reduced blood pressure and stress. In addition, people who engage in "forest bathing" report feeling more attuned with their intuition, increased ability to communicate with the planet and with other species, deepening friendships, and increases in sensing their own life force and happiness.

5. *Greater perspective taking*: Your toxic relationship has caused you much difficulty and suffering, but when you lie on your back and look at the stars, or climb a mountain and look at a verdant vista, your own problems can begin to seem small and your sense of wonder can become vast. Time outside supports a sense of wonder.

You don't need to go hike the Grand Canyon to receive the benefits of getting outside. Even brief walks in the city prove beneficial, if you use them as opportunities to experience weather, enjoy plants and animals and water, and connect with the world around you. If you can spend time in less urban environments, take your shoes off, and cultivate relationships with your local trees or gardens or water, all the better. If you are driving between three part-time jobs and your kid's school, feeling that you are barely holding things together as you create your recovery, consider pulling the car over for a restoration break in that park or waterfront or roadside rest on your route.

The goal of spending time outside as part of your ESC plan is, quite literally, to help you ground yourself, to feel more centered and connected, and to support your health and happiness.

Elevate your heart rate

As part of your ESC plan, I encourage you to indulge your body in some exercise that elevates your heart rate. If you run or race bikes or dance Zumba, you already know why! If you spend most of your time at a desk or commuting in a car between desks as you try to take care of your life post-narcissist, it's especially important that you honor your body by giving yourself the opportunity to move vigorously on a regular basis. You don't have to devote a dedicated hour to exercise every day if this is too much for your schedule right now, but you can find ways to include some cardio challenge in your current environment in short bursts. Indeed, some trainers suggest short bursts of exercise several times a day may have greater benefits than living a sedentary lifestyle punctuated by visits to the gym. You might start by climbing a couple of flights of stairs at work or at home or outside somewhere, walking up a hill on a break, or working in some dancing or jumping jacks as you go about your day — all of these elevate your heart rate. If you are able to work in a game of soccer or a run, that's great too.

Exercise that elevates our heart rates gives us a number of benefits. It decreases our resting heart rates, which is seen as a sign of improved cardiac health. It supports the immune system. It seems to flush toxins from the body. It supports becoming or staying at a healthy weight. It supports our self-esteem. And, because of the endorphin rush associated with vigorous exercise, it leaves us feeling energized and alive. In the wake of a toxic relationship that has left you feeling depleted, exhausted, discouraged, or overwhelmed, vigorous exercise, even in very short bursts, can play an important role in reminding yourself how good it is to be alive and in sending the message to your spirit that positive change is happening and you are moving forward.

You don't need an expensive gym membership or fancy equipment or a personal trainer to include vigorous exercise in your regular routine — though a great gym, an enthusiastic trainer, and nice equipment can be wonderful! Start in ways that are manageable for you, and expand from there, as time, resources, and enthusiasm allow. Keep it simple and connected to how you already live and what you already enjoy, if this will be new territory for you. If you join a gym, make it one close to where you live or work. If you hire a personal trainer, make sure you feel a connection to them. Use free online resources, such as those at Sparkpeople.com, to think about ways to integrate exercise into your regular environment, including at your desk. If joining a gym feels beyond your reach, contact your local YMCA; many have policies that say nobody is turned away based on ability to pay.

The better you feel physically, the more physically ready you will feel to take on all of the challenges that this recovery requires of you. In the process, you will be creating your best health and best life possible.

Energetic reset

Although I'm trained as a social scientist and a therapist — or perhaps because of this — I believe that much of our human experience is not yet captured, well-described, or understood through the frameworks of contemporary science and medicine.

As you deal with a disordered person, for example, you may have the feeling that you can anticipate their next move, or that they can anticipate yours. To some extent, this can be explained by observation and using the past to predict the future, but there's often a degree of "psychic connection" we feel with people we love or people with whom we are entangled (or both) that goes beyond simple familiarity. When we are around people who are good to us and good for us, we feel good — happy, energized, relaxed. When we are around people who are toxic for us, our energy becomes depleted, uneven, and misdirected. Consider incorporating in your recovery some practices designed to restore balance and vivaciousness in your energy system.

Many healing traditions across the world have developed understandings of the energy of the body. Chinese and Japanese acupuncture work with the body's meridians or energy pathways; the yogic traditions of India address the energy vortexes called chakras; and Celtic traditions conceptualize the body's energy as contained inside a master grid. Energy healer Donna Eden, author of the book *Energy Medicine* (2008), describes each of these understandings as true – and each as constituting one element of an integrated system. Other traditions use facets of these elements or related systems of our energetic make-up in their approaches to healing. The goal of each of them, however, is to remove barriers that are blocking energetic pathways, to clean out emotional and energetic "waste," to balance energy across the systems, and to promote healing.

Acupuncture and reiki are increasingly well-known approaches to energy medicine in the West. I encourage you to explore each of them. Ask people for referrals to good practitioners in your area, and give yourself several sessions before determining if the work helps you. If you cannot yet afford to see professional practitioners, you might want to learn energy self-care practices that you can incorporate into your daily Exquisite Self Care program. Some of these could include learning acupressure, studying Eden Energy Medicine, or learning t'ai chi, a moving meditation and martial art. Meditation, conscious breathing, and yoga also all can contribute to resetting your energy — and all of these can be done in small doses, short bursts, in small spaces, and for free.

Massage

One of our first experiences in the world is to be received into welcoming hands.

Although many of us have complicated relationships with the touch — or lack of touch — we experience after that first amazing passage into the hands that catch us as we arrive here, the truth is that humans, like all mammals, need to touch and be touched.

Your relationship with touch may have been complex before your relationship with your toxic partner, but it is likely that your relationship has made it worse. It may be that although you have been in a close relationship, your partner may have withdrawn touch, so you may be extremely touch-deprived. It may be that your partner used sexual touch to manipulate you and keep you in the relationship for longer than you would have stayed otherwise, so now you are experiencing withdrawal, not only of sex but also of touch in general. It may be that your toxic partner used touch as a weapon, hurting you or threatening to use physical force against you Whether touch or the withdrawal of touch was used to manipulate you in your relationship, the bottom line is that it is important to shift your relationship with touch in a healthy direction — and to take steps to ensure that healthy touch is a regular part of your life as you recover.

We may receive welcome touch from friends and family members, but most of us in the wake of a difficult emotional experience can benefit from more. Recent research documents how healthy touch improves the immune system, the functioning of the brain, and even the body's blood pressure and pulse; the former three of these tend to fall into alignment with the person touching us, so it's important that we engage in physical contact with people who are calm and positive. One way of incorporating healthy touch into your life is to arrange for therapeutic massage.

There are many ways to incorporate massage into your life:

One is to engage in self-massage. Think about your natural reaction to accidentally injuring yourself. Often it is to rub the spot of the injury. This is a nearly automatic response among humans — because it feels good, reduces pain, and provides self-soothing. You can touch yourself in a soothing way without the excuse of an injury. Self-massage has many of the same benefits of receiving massage from others. Some people make it a habit to use self-massage as part of their wake-up routine. Try this for three days and see how you feel about it.

Another strategy is to swap massage treatments informally with friends or family members. You can deliver wonderful massages on the floor or bed, or while the beneficiary is seated. You may even want to purchase a massage table for this purpose (used ones are abundant on Craig's List); if you know a couple of friends who would do massage exchange with you, the price of the table would easily be outdistanced by the money you are saving by sharing massage with friends. This is doubly beneficial because you are not only receiving but giving, which is both physically and emotionally helpful to you.

Finally, you may want to hire a professional for therapeutic massage. Generally, you should find a massage therapist by asking for recommendations from trusted friends and family members. When you interview a massage therapist, it's helpful to ask where they went to school and to make sure they are licensed to practice. If you find the rates in your vicinity difficult to afford at present, consider contacting local massage schools; they often have a student clinic you can visit for services at a much reduced rate in recognition that the therapist you will see is still a student. While it is ideal to work with a trained therapist you like over the course of time, so that they get to know your body and can give you feedback on changes, working with multiple therapists at a student clinic is still a good option, and it may be a good way to cultivate a relationship with a new therapist at the beginning of their career.

Mammals of all species, humans included, need regular touch with respect and kindness. Make it an explicit goal on your ESC plan that you will have at least one full minute of physical contact with another mammal every day.

Cultivate your spirit

Relationships with narcissists and other toxic characters dampen your spirit. Although your toxic Ex chose you because of your lovely soul, they proceeded to try to destroy it — either because it brought them pleasure to have the upper hand or because protecting your spirit was not a priority for them. Part of the task ahead of you is to restore your own spirit.

Here, I'd like to contribute to that process by encouraging you to finish the following sentences:

1. Before this relationship, I would describe my spirit as:
2. When I was a child, my spirit was:
3. I have always been most in touch with my spirit when:
4. The natural element that my spirit reminds me of is:
5. My spirit feels most free when I:

Now, identify three actions to put yourself back in touch with your spirit.

Three things I can do to put myself back in touch with my spirit:
1.
2.
3.

These will, of course, be different for everyone. For one person, it might be flying down a hill on a bike, while for another it might be singing country tunes as loud as they can. For one of my clients, it was shoveling out horse stalls; for another, it was dancing. Whatever it is for you should be on your self-care agenda.

If you'd like to delve a little deeper into this, you might want to consult someone who has special skills in helping people get in touch with their spirits or with lost parts of their souls. Some shamanistic healers from various traditions do "soul retrieval," "soul calling," or "soul journeying" work, offer sweat lodges or Zen retreats, or provide pastoral counseling. All of these approaches can have benefits to people seeking a deeper experience of their spirits, in the hands of competent (that's important!) and trustworthy guides.

However you go about reconnecting with your spirit and reclaiming your true self, trust that it can be done, and that your lovely spirit deserves to be whole and happy.

Vision boards

Even if you aren't "the crafty type," you can benefit from the process of creating a vision board. Vision boards can help people clarify their desires, refine their plans, and bring into the material world ideas you have about your best life possible.

The idea of a vision board, at its most simple, is this: you'll make a physical representation of what you would like to bring into your life. This can be done in many ways, and however you do it will be better than not doing it at all. You can make a vision board in a very simple way, using a piece of paper and something to write or draw with, or make your vision board as elaborate as a wall in your home that becomes a living collage featuring words and images of the future you are moving into.

In general, the process is this: dedicate some time to this project, knowing that you can continue to revise the vision board as time goes on. Devote some paper or a bulletin board, or a wall, or some other surface to serving as the vision board. Sit quietly for a few moments, centering yourself on the question of what you would like to experience/do/have in the short term and the long term of your life — perhaps defining your vision for the next six months, year, five years, and ten years. Connect here with your best possible vision of your life, setting aside what you understand to be its limitations, deficits, or difficulties. What we're going for here is a connection to your deepest, sweetest, perhaps wildest dreams. They all are welcome here.

Now, begin to work on your board. If you aren't artsy, and feel more at home in the world of words than the world of images, you may wish to begin your vision board by writing words on it. If you are more visual than verbal, you may wish to start drawing images that represent your vision. You may wish to draw images and write words in combination. There aren't bonus points for perfection or artistic merit! What we're working on here is making a space for your vision of a great future to be expressed outside of your head, and for you to become more in touch with your desires. For a more elaborate vision board, you may want to cut out images or words from magazines or print out online images – for example, of places in the world you would like to see.

Let go of the urge to limit yourself to what seems possible — your mind has been well-trained to raise objections to your dreams, hopes, and desires. Don't worry about the "how's" for now; focus instead on the "what's" —what you would like to be experiencing, doing, and having in your ideal life. Some areas to think about are: relationships, work, living situations, health, travel, money, adventure, generosity to others, pastimes, community, creativity, feelings, goals, achievements, and time. There are many ways to think about our existence here, many ways to value different aspects and experiences of being alive. Your vision board is uniquely yours; design, organize, and create it in a way that feels like an expression of who you are – and who you are becoming.

When the first phase of your vision board project feels complete, install the board somewhere in your home or workspace. If you are in transition and your vision board needs to be kept small so that it's easily transported, that's okay, too – just know where it is. Many people discover that the process of creating a vision board works a kind of magic in their lives that is effortless beyond creating the board; once someone has created a vision board that includes "more exercise," they suddenly have people giving them bikes or inviting them to join a team or work out at a gym. Of course, when these opportunities arise, it's important to do your best to step up on your side of things. "Oh! I asked the universe for this — here it is! I'm going to say yes — and thank you!" Continue to update your vision board. Often, you will be amazed at how this process helps you create the best life you can envision, how quickly what you envision becomes real, and how soon you will need to expand your vision once again as you move into your best life possible.

Journaling

I have always been fond of the paraphrase of an E.M. Forster quote about the power of writing to clarify our thinking: "How do I know what I think till I see what I say?"

Keeping a journal helps you during your recovery from a toxic relationship in a number of ways. You can use a journal to vent your feelings and frustrations, to work out your response to challenges that arise, to make plans and visions for the future, and to create a pathway to insight on the personal pre-history that may have made you vulnerable to a toxic relationship. Journaling over the course of time allows you to create a living document that you may use to reflect on the changes in your life, as you map how you were doing two years ago, six months ago, and last week, and how your life has improved as you have taken the reigns of your wellbeing.

There are no right and wrong ways to journal. You don't need to buy a special journal to get started – although some people enjoy having a journal that feels and looks different from other kinds of notebooks and logs. Some people keep their journal online, in the form of a blog. Although this can be helpful and satisfying, I also encourage you to spend regular time writing by hand. The connection between our emotions and handwriting seems to be different from the connection between typing and our emotions, and may give you deeper access to the most intuitive parts of yourself. It may feel awkward or uncomfortable at first to express your thoughts and feelings in writing, knowing that the only audience for this work is likely to be yourself. That's okay. Hang with it. Develop a regular journal practice — whether you write a little every day or give yourself a weekly journal check-in time for a few months. Like vision boards, journals represent a connection between the invisible world of feelings, thoughts, intuition, and dreams, and the material world in which we bring our thoughts to action and form. Developing a regular journal practice allows you to tell your life story as it unfolds – and also to create your life story by anticipating, in writing, the new shapes it can take as you move forward in your less encumbered life.

Freedom rituals

Whether you consider yourself religious or spiritual-but-not-religious or neither of these, you may benefit from using ritual elements to mark your freedom from an unhealthy relationship. Rituals are connected to rites-of-passage, special events or ceremonies that mark our transition from one status to another, such as from one age to another on birthdays, from childhood to adulthood on bat and bar mitzvahs, from single to married at weddings, or from married to divorced in court hearings, though the rituals of legal proceedings usually have fewer personal elements and are less responsive to the personal beliefs and styles of the people involved.

Some letting go/clearing out/ending rituals are remarkably simple, such as that of a man I know who climbed a very tall hill, said a few words to the universe regarding his letting go of a toxic marriage, removed his wedding ring, tossed it down the far side of the hill, and clambered down again a free man. Other letting go rituals look more involved. For instance, you may wish to gather friends together to mark the end of this challenging time in your relationship life. You may simply make an announcement about your commitment to reclaiming your life and invite people to help you remember the things you have enjoyed doing with them over the course of time. You could ask someone symbolically to bind your hands with crepe paper and then witness you breaking out of those binds.

Water and fire are used in many traditions as part of ritual work, so consider whether you want to write a letter to your Ex and toss it into a moving body of water, to write a list of painful things that have happened in your relationship and burn it so that the painful experiences can be released, or to build a fire on a beach, reflect on the good, bad, and confusing about your relationship, make a commitment to being free and recovering, and let the fire burn down until you douse it with water.

Sometimes people find it helpful consciously to include good wishes for their toxic partners in letting go rituals. Recognizing that a person isn't good for you doesn't mean you need to wish them harm or pain. It can be soothing to wish the person well as they move forward, even though they could not relate to you from a place of integrity. You may consider saying out loud, chanting, or praying "I release you and wish you well. May you be happy, may you be free," even as you may repeat for yourself, "May I be well. May I be free. May I be happy."

Because we all have unique histories and because relationships are unique, how you choose to mark your rite of passage from in-a-toxic-situation to free-from-a-toxic-situation can also be unique. Even so, it can also connect you to the greater flow of life and allow you symbolically to reinforce for yourself that you are no longer willing to be in relationships in which you are exploited or abused. Human beings have created rituals for thousands of years to bring ourselves peace and to help us move from one status to another. That human legacy can help you in the process you are undertaking now.

Shift your moods

Your situation is difficult, no doubt about it. If your mood is in the tank, it's not surprising. You may wonder how you got snookered into a crazy relationship, whether you will ever be able to be free of it, how you will dig yourself out of any financial or legal trouble it created, and whether you will ever have a healthy, happy relationship. All of these kinds of questions can leave you feeling pretty somber. You may even feel that you can't give yourself permission to lighten up, or that lightening up is impossible, given the radical circumstances.

I'm going to encourage you to think differently about this.

By claiming radical responsibility for your situation, circumstances, and mood, you create the possibility of changing all of them. If you are responsible for your mood, you can shift it. Taking responsibility for your mood doesn't mean living in denial about what unfortunate thing your partner may have done to create misery for you — your partner's behavior is their responsibility, and you get to make decisions about how you will respond to them. So, you can respond to hurtful behavior in effective ways and still give yourself permission to shift your own mood. In essence, hold them accountable for their behavior, but hold yourself responsible for your own emotional state, well-being, and mood.

How might you shift out of a difficult mood?

First, get curious and be kind with yourself using these possible steps:

1. Identify the thought that is beneath the mood, such as "I don't know how I will ever pay off the debt I took on in this relationship."
2. Explore whether there's a more productive way of working with this, such as asking a question like, "How can I go about paying off this debt?" and staying with this line of thinking.
3. Offer yourself some reassurance: "I am a smart person and I work hard, so even though this is difficult, I will find a way to address it."
4. Return to the present moment. "Even though this debt is a big problem, I don't have to solve it all right now. I can see that in this moment, I am someplace safe, the weather is good, and I can be kind to myself."

Second, there are many active practices that you can use to shift your mood. Here are ten:

1. Listen to or play music
2. Sing or chant
3. Engage in physical activity: walk, run, dance, skip
4. Take a shower or bath
5. Go outside and play
6. Interact with babies, children, pets, or plants
7. Call a friend
8. Drink a glass of water
9. Make art
10. Read a book

As you gain experience in taking responsibility and care for your moods, you will feel more empowered and come to see that while your toxic partner may have caused trouble and pain for you, you still have the power to determine your own emotional reality, no matter what is coming your way. You will also be less likely to blame yourself (and others). Blame is pointless, harmful, and unproductive, whereas holding ourselves and others accountable for actions is profoundly powerful.

Laughing matters

When was the last time you laughed so hard you had trouble catching your breath? Life can get awfully serious when you are dealing with the fallout of a difficult relationship. Even though some of us can hold onto a wry or ironic sense of humor in the midst of toxic relationship trouble, lighthearted laughter can sometimes seem a thing of the past. As you become more fully committed to your recovery and to reclaiming your happiness, I hope you will accept this assignment: find ways to laugh your tush off.

We have been conditioned to think that we need to see or hear something funny in order to enjoy a good laugh, but the truth is that we can laugh just for the sake of it. Some people call this "laughing meditation," and it feels good. Yes, you have permission to laugh right now, even though nothing funny is going on. Try it. As you start, it will probably feel awkward, but if you keep going you will eventually pick up momentum and find yourself laughing naturally. Laughing is good for our souls, our hearts, our immune systems, and our psyches. It's important to get back to it.

Of course, there are many ways to trigger laughing besides just deciding to do it. Do you have a favorite funny video or movie? Is there a stand-up comedy club near you? Do you always laugh when you see kittens tumbling? Do you have a friend who always makes you laugh? Do you remember websites or YouTube videos that crack you up? Make a conscious effort to seek out people, events, and media you know will make you laugh, and do your best to give yourself over to laughter when you feel it arising. You may be out of practice, but with a little opportunity, your laughing habit will be restored.

Take things into your own hands

Until a few decades ago, people in North America still were making their own lives better by using their own hands to practice practical skills: sewing, farming or gardening, making or repairing furniture and household appliances, making, mending, and washing clothes, chopping wood, repairing their cars and farm equipment, tending animals, and, of course, cooking. People also used their hands more for three-dimensional hobbies and pastimes, some of which had practical applications: quilting, making and playing instruments, painting, building tree houses. In the information age, we have made the mistake of assuming that convenience would lead to greater happiness, but in the process have lost many practical skills. It's interesting that research now suggests that those very "inconvenient" old school activities actually support our happiness: the human brain evolved to connect pleasure with accomplishing things with our hands. As we make less and do less with our hands, we may have set ourselves up for increased rates of depression and lower feelings of self-worth.

What does this have to do with your recovery from a toxic relationship?

As you recover, it's important to do everything you can to support your happiness, positive mood, and sense of well-being. For too long, you have over-focused on someone else's welfare, over-worked to take care of them, or lived in fear and frustration. The practices here are designed to help you recharge and rediscover the delightful ways you can experience the world. One of those ways may well be found in getting back to—or discovering—how good it feels to change the world with the intentional use of your hands. So: consider taking a glass-blowing class, or devote two nights a week to cooking, or learn how to change a bike tire and practice it 100 times, until you feel competent at it. Take up knitting and make yourself a blanket, basking in the warmth that you discover you can create for yourself. Learn cross-stitch or buy a few blank canvases and make new art for your home. Refinish a piece of furniture. Plant bulbs. Don't just cruise Pinterest: make something happen.

All of these projects will engage your hands, your creativity, and your self-satisfaction. They will also slow things down a bit, allowing you time "outside of your head" to concentrate on the simple details of a project that improves your life, beautifies your home, or evolves into gifts you give others…all of which supports your happiness and sense of self-care.

Remembering yourself

Often, as I become familiar with the life histories of clients exiting or recovering from relationships with toxic partners, I am struck by how stunningly talented, competent, and resilient they are — and by how out of touch with their own power they have become. I have learned that the narcissist, psychopath, or person with borderline traits chose you for a reason — likely because you have not only the temperament but also the skills, resources, and qualities that they need to meet their goals – but do not themselves possess.

Perhaps you connect well with people, are devoted and loyal, have business acumen or the ability to manage finances, special knowledge about a particular field, or a creative bent that allows you to solve problems, thrive in hostile climates, or make money in new and unexpected ways. The toxic person chose you because of your strengths, talents, and skills because these could make their life easier, move them toward their goals, or help them look good — indeed, help them look much better than they are.

Unfortunately, the exploitation you've experienced has probably undermined your sense of your own capacities and self-worth; that, too, is part of the strategy toxic personalities use. Now that you are exiting, it's time to put yourself back in touch with your own best self, even when that best self feels like a distant memory. Trust me: your skills, talents, and core strengths are still there, waiting to be rediscovered and valued by you.

Here's a very small exercise to get you started:

While you're thinking about it, put a notebook or calendar and something to write with next to where you sleep.

At the end of the day, write down three things you did today that you're proud of, that you did well, or that you feel good about. The goal here is to begin to re-notice your goodness, strengths, and talents.

Do this for one month. Each night, write down three things you like about yourself, and review what you have written on the other nights. Bit by bit, you will begin to rebuild your confidence in your strength, kindness, resilience, and capacity to persevere.

Post-crisis therapy and support

As you enter and move through the process of recovering from a toxic relationship, you may find it beneficial to enlist the aid of counselors, therapists, and other healers, including spiritual guides such as rabbis, ministers, Buddhist teachers, shamans, and medicine people. In my position as a therapist working with people on this journey, the goals of therapy and support at this stage include:

1. Helping you to calm your nervous system and reclaim your wellbeing.
2. Helping you to relax into a life in which contact with the narcissist is eliminated or minimized.
3. Helping you to create the best life possible for yourself now.
4. Helping you to explore the vulnerabilities that your toxic Ex exploited and to heal these to reduce your vulnerability to exploitation in the future.
5. Helping you to prepare to love and trust again in whatever ways you desire for yourself.

It may be useful for you to work with people from several traditions on your path to accomplishing these goals. Seeing your experience from multiple perspectives as you make meaning of it can be very beneficial. Here are some questions to ask practitioners or clinicians you consider consulting:

1. What have been your experiences working with survivors of toxic relationships?
2. What healing techniques do you bring to your work with people who have experienced trauma?
3. What kind of outcomes or benefits do people usually experience when they work on trauma issues with you?

I focus on trauma here because nearly everyone who has survived a toxic relationship carries some wounds from it; these need to be healed so that you can live your best, most vibrant life possible. Working with trauma-savvy therapists, counselors, healers, and consultants who understand the complexities of relationships with people with personality disorders will increase the resources available to you as you recover.

One treatment approach used by psychotherapists that you may find especially beneficial is called Eye Movement Desensitization and Reprocessing (EMDR). Discovered and developed by Francine Shapiro, Ph.D., EMDR is a non-invasive protocol for relieving the emotional charge of self-blaming thoughts associated with traumatic memories. We use it with firefighters, police officers, and veterans, as well as with survivors of rape and incest, domestic violence, and child abuse. Many times it proves to be both gentler and faster in relieving the suffering of people who have experienced traumatic interpersonal situations.

Sometimes, people who haven't gotten much relief from several years of conventional psychotherapy experience great reductions in their suffering and increases in their feelings of ease and wellbeing after three or four sessions of EMDR. As you move through your recovery process, adding an EMDR trained therapist to your team of trauma-sensitive practitioners may accelerate the pace at which you heal. And a bonus: because our vulnerabilities to toxic people are often rooted in the old traumas and hurts that are addressed by EMDR, EMDR will relieve some of the pain of your toxic relationships and also reduce your vulnerability to difficult relationships in the future.

Alchemy

In the wake of toxic relationships, there's often a trail of toxic artifacts. Some of those artifacts are actual physical objects. They themselves may not be toxic, but the feelings that come up for you when you see them may get in the way of your recovery by keeping the wounds open. In this practice, you will make a conscious decision to let go of these artifacts in the interest of eliminating them as triggers for your suffering. Whenever possible, you will use them to create happiness for yourself and others — that's the power of transformational magic.

Let's imagine that your former partner had a challenging habit of misspending money on technological gadgets, and that this had been a source of conflict for you. Now, you are stuck with a big screen TV that you neither want nor use. It takes up space in your home. Every time you see this TV, you feel frustration and anger come up in you as you remember conflicts about its purchase and think about the money that was spent on it over your objection.

In order to practice transformational magic, you will need to take action: you will need to get the TV out of your house, and do so in a way that brings good to someone else. For example, instead of just putting the TV on the curb or destroying it, you could call a local charity that runs a thrift shop and have them pick it up and sell it in their store —— essentially making the TV a gift to charity that will also be tax deductible for you. You could also consider donating the TV to a group that will use it — a local clubhouse for cancer survivors or a teen meet-up space, or a social fraternity or a religious or community organization. Imagine groups of people enjoying the TV together, socializing, and appreciating your generosity. Imagine beginning to feel good about having turned the television into a gift that others benefit from and give you gratitude for, even as you free up your own space and eliminate this painful reminder. This is the heart of transformational magic and alchemy.

Some artifacts from your toxic relationship simply can go into the dumpster; some you may need to hold onto (someplace out-of-sight) for the purposes of documentation; but most can be sources of transformational magic that will allow you to feel lighter, connect with people who will reflect your generosity back to you through gratitude, and allow you to turn something that has been a source of pain for you into a source of pleasure for others.

Today is a perfect day to enact transformation.

Space makeover

Now that you have practiced transformational magic and decluttered the material triggers that remind you of your toxic relationship, consider re-claiming, re-designing, and re-envisioning your living space.

Perhaps you made a lot of space for your Ex that you can reclaim. Perhaps your Ex-used space in your shared home in ways that you didn't enjoy. Perhaps you have a vision of activities you'd like to do in your home that you weren't able to do until now because of the demands of your difficult relationship or its structural requirements. Perhaps you've been too exhausted to do any household maintenance for months, or too depressed to clean.

Now's the time.

Think about the most holy, majestic, and inspiring built spaces you've ever entered. What do they have in common? What have you appreciated most about them?

Think of the coziest, warmest, friendliest spaces you've ever enjoyed. What did they have in common? What did you enjoy most about them?

What kind of space would you most enjoy living in? What would its essential qualities be, no matter how large or small it is?

Your task now is to create a space that you love and that loves you back, one in which you feel nurtured and comfortable, one that inspires your creativity, joy, and peace.

What changes do you need to make to achieve the qualities of space you value? Often, these elements can be achieved for very little expense; the important thing is to have a vision of the kind of space in which you feel happy — and to have the belief that you deserve to live in a space that supports your peacefulness, comfort, and joy.

If you feel overwhelmed by housekeeping, you might visit Flylady.com for incredible support for overwhelmed housekeepers. If you need assistance with letting go of unnecessary stuff, you might benefit from reading around at theminimialists.com. If you need ideas for redesigning your space, making art, or using the space available to you differently, you can find abundant online resources. You may also have handy friends who would be happy to help you re-paint, to repurpose your stuff, to join you in an art-making party, or to go thrifting with you to find just what you need, once you have your vision dialed in.

The goal of reclaiming your space is to increase your comfort and ease, your peacefulness and joy, your ability to have what you want and need in the most intimate of spaces beyond your body. Whether what you want and need is solitude in a home that is a lovely retreat, or company in a home that is welcoming to friends and family, creating it or reclaiming it is an outward manifestation of your interior world. As you recover from a toxic relationship, having surroundings that honor and support that lovely interior will help it to re-emerge.

Self-defense and assertiveness

When you contemplate how things unfolded in your troublesome relationship, you probably recall moments when you wish you had stood up better for yourself, asserted yourself more clearly, had better boundaries, or refused to accept exploitative, manipulative, or abusive behavior. If this is true for you, it's probable that you came into the relationship with a skill deficit in this area — whether because you come from a childhood in which you weren't supported in having good boundaries and effective assertiveness, or because you have never encountered someone who had an agenda of exploiting you, so you hadn't before had the need to use your skills so assertively.

Now is a perfect time to develop or fine-tune your assertiveness and self-defense skills, because doing so will allow you to feel more confident and safe in the present, and more confident, comfortable, and skillful in the future. When you trust that you are worth taking care of, and are confident in your own ability to take care of yourself, you are far less likely to get entangled with people who will take advantage of you. The goal of self-defense and assertiveness training is not to make you aggressive, but instead to help you have skills that let you carry yourself confidently in the world. Because self-defense and assertiveness training involves training both the body and the mind, it helps people go beyond "getting it" at a conscious level; it allows you really to integrate into your physical body the message that you can — and will — take care of yourself.

There are many places to take self-defense and assertiveness training. If training in the martial arts appeals to you, you can explore local dojos or martial arts studios that teach karate, tai kwon do, aikido, or a host of other forms. Undertaking long-term training in martial arts is very beneficial physically, emotionally, and cognitively. Nonetheless, you don't need to make a long-term commitment to get the basic principles and benefits of practical self-defense and assertiveness training; there exist many opportunities to take short courses that will offer you many benefits. These are often offered through local rape crisis agencies, through colleges and universities that will allow you to enroll as a special student in the physical fitness department, and through community recreation and YMCA/YWCA programming. Ask around for recommendations. I am especially fond of feminist-theory based self-defense courses because they offer an analysis of the social organization of power and exploitation, but many programs that don't advertise feminist roots have a similar foundation that will help you look at the broader systems of inequality that allow abusive people to identify prospective victims.

Each one teach one

You probably know the standard reasons therapists recommend volunteer work: it connects us to others, helps us keep our own lives in perspective, and makes us feel good about making someone else's life better.

For survivors of relationships with narcissists, volunteering can be beneficial for additional reasons, especially if you volunteer in an environment dedicated to helping people who have been exploited, bullied, or abused, who are experiencing mental health crises (for example, are calling suicide hotlines), or who are dealing with or recovering from some other sort of social difficulty. Working with others in these environments has a number of benefits:

1. It allows you to begin to see the strategies that narcissists use to exploit their victims.
2. It allows you to begin to see your own vulnerability to toxic people more clearly.
3. It allows you to support others in identifying, resisting, rejecting, and recovering from narcissistic abuse.
4. It allows you to become stronger in your own resolve to keep your life clear of exploitation.

As you become stronger, freer, and clearer, you may be inspired to use your own special skills and gifts to help others who have suffered as a result of their involvement with toxic partners, parents, children, or colleagues. Perhaps you have accounting, financial management, legal, writing, counseling, group leadership, ritual design, spiritual, or medicinal training or talents that you can offer specifically to others surviving and recovering from exploitative relationships. Using your strengths to help others and to make the world a better place often becomes a far more rewarding and productive use of your time and talent than continuing to pursue justice from your own exploitative former partner, and one more strategy for transforming your difficult experience into a gift to others and to yourself.

Shall we dance?

Intuitively, you might expect self-defense, yoga and meditation, and general endorphin-inducing exercise to be among my recommended recovery practices, but feel surprised to see social dance show up here. Yet, I enthusiastically recommend taking up social dance as part of your recovery. I'm a particular fan of ballroom dances, Argentine tango, and the Latin dances, such as salsa and rumba, but any dance that involves a partner (hello country two-step!) and that appeals to you will be a great choice.

Social dance provides opportunities for many beneficial experiences: it lets us make gentle physical and social contact with others in pleasant, affirming environments. It is governed by some formal guidelines for the etiquette of interactions. And it gives people opportunities to practice leading and following in balanced ways. As a survivor of a crazy-making relationship, you have experienced imbalance in your partnership. Through the experience of learning to lead or follow — or both, in the best case scenario — you will have an opportunity to re-learn how to be responsive without taking too much responsibility, how to provide leadership that is neither too meek nor too controlling, and, ultimately, how to dance in ways that keep you centered in your own body and experience while connecting with someone else who does the same. Through social dance, you have an embodied way of experiencing what feels good in contact with someone else — when the connection feels fluid and balanced and secure, when it feels controlling or overpowering, and when your dance partner isn't stepping up to contribute a fair share to making the dance a happy, interesting, comfortable experience. As you become more skilled at dancing with partners – and I suggest you practice with many — social dance can become a profound metaphor for the broader dynamics in your relationships, and one that you can use as a template for the kind of relationships you hope to have from here forward.

Besides all that, it's a lot of fun.

Reconnecting

Time in a toxic relationship can wreak havoc on your social life for a number of reasons:

- Your toxic partner may have pressured you to cut ties with or keep your distance from friends and family members.
- Friends and family members may have given you the signal that they don't want to hear from you while you are still involved with your toxic partner.
- The financial demands of the relationship have kept you over-working, so that your availability to socialize has been reduced dramatically.
- You have been too ashamed to share what has been going on in your relationship with other people, cutting down on your closeness to them.
- The demands of the relationship have been so great that you have lost both time and energy for connecting with others.

It's time to make a concerted effort to reconnect in the Land of the Living.

Humans are social animals. Although some can manage without human contact for lengths of time, most of us do better when we have social connections. These can be of varying degrees of intimacy, but they need to involve kindness, reciprocity, and a sense of care.

You can go about re-establishing a social life in a number of ways. One is to reach out to people from whom you have become distant as a result of your toxic relationship. You can let them know that you are sorry your relationship got in the way of your friendship with them and that you would like to repair things and move forward. Many friends and family members are very pleased to hear that someone they care about has decided to exit a toxic romance, and will greet you with welcome and relief. Another approach is to create new friendships totally unconnected to your toxic partner or relationship. The value of new friendships is that they don't have to be infused with the drama and crises of your toxic partnership;

essentially, you begin them with a clean slate. It's up to you, as you get to know people, to decide what you want to share about what you have been through, but you don't have to lead with it. You can allow people to get to know you and enjoy you on your own terms, which can be very therapeutic in itself, and which helps you to become more and more grounded in the present and oriented toward the future, rather than stuck and isolated because of the pain and drama of the past.

Animal love

Humans are, of course animals, and we share the planet with animals of other species in a web of inter-dependence and complex relationships. Many humans have found great pleasure and emotional meaning in cultivating relationships with animals of other species. As you recover from a difficult relationship with a difficult human being, connecting with an animal of another species may offer much in the way of opportunities to express caring, to receive affection, to feel connection, and to practice peaceful co-existence with others.

You're probably familiar with the concept of therapy animals and helper animals – a testimony to the value that many of us place on animals' abilities to help humans heal — both through their own capacities and as we experience the benefits of caring for them.

In the United States, many companion animals are available for adoption from shelters and rescue programs. If you have never lived with an animal before, you may wish to do some research about animal roommates. Most animal shelters and rescues can help you explore the kind of pet that would be best suited for your lifestyle, housing situation, and financial resources, and give you helpful guidance as you move toward bringing an animal into your life.

If you are not in a situation that allows you to adopt an animal at present, consider volunteering at an animal shelter or sanctuary, or even at a stable or farm. Regular contact with animals, and knowing that you are improving the welfare of another sentient being, can help you feel more connected to others, improve your mood, increase your physical health, and offer you an opportunity to be in a relationship that has a dynamic of mutual positive regard. An animal friend will not say harsh or cruel things to you, exploit you financially, or cheat on you. They may, however, introduce you to other human beings who like animals. Wouldn't it be nice to know more of those?

Gratitude

You may be feeling depleted, frustrated, and exploited. You may be feeling angry, disillusioned, and worried. You may be feeling afraid, agitated, and exhausted. And in the midst of this, I am going to ask you to practice gratitude. Practicing gratitude may be the most essential recovery skill I can encourage you to cultivate.

Making a commitment to practicing gratitude will bring you many benefits. By practicing gratitude —consciously finding things to be thankful for in your life — you will begin to counteract the negative emotional states that may dominate your interior world. Practicing gratitude doesn't require that you see the world through rose-colored glasses or deny the very real difficulties that you have experienced or are now facing, but it does broaden your perspective, help you appreciate the good things in your life, and help you cultivate hope.

We rarely know in advance how most things will turn out. Our greatest challenges sometimes cultivate our greatest strengths and lead us into new territory that we would never have explored if we hadn't been required to find creative solutions. In the aftermath of a financial disaster, you may create a way of making money that turns out to be a great source of fulfillment. In the wake of being cheated on, you may find yourself single and available to meet the true love of your life. In response to a relationship with a toxic partner, you may become very good at screening future prospects and holding out for one who can see you clearly and appreciate you deeply. If you are feeling down and out, neglected, dejected, rejected, and abused, the experience that landed you here may, in the end, turn out to be the most valuable learning experience of your life.

So, begin to cultivate gratitude. You could be grateful that the relationship is finally over, that you finally see it clearly, and that the road ahead will give you more (or total) freedom from your abusive partner. You could be grateful that you have more peace on a daily basis now. You can also be grateful for what you have learned from this relationship, for the new path that you are setting for yourself, and for the steps you are making for your recovery. More broadly, find things to be grateful for such as your friends and family, your work or school or prospects, a place to live, access to food. Even more broadly, you can be grateful for sunrises and sunsets, for weather, for water, for air.

Keeping a gratitude journal or devoting a portion of your journaling work to expressing gratitude begins to build a gratitude habit. It's wonderful to feel gratitude throughout your day, and by writing down each day what you are grateful for, you will begin to cultivate a greater awareness of your good fortune, your strengths, and the beauty around you. This, in turn, will help you interrupt the cycles of negative thinking, difficult moods, pessimism, and despair often present in recovery from narcissistic abuse. By discovering, rediscovering, or cultivating your optimism and resilience through cultivating gratitude, you move your life forward, become more in touch with your creativity, and attract into your life others who see the world through the a similar lens.

BEGINNING ANEW

In each ending lie the seeds of new beginnings. I hope this small book has helped you clarify how to create your best life possible, how to make yourself available to the goodness of love and kindness, and how to recover — from the traumas that may have made you vulnerable to a toxic relationship, from the difficulties of the relationship itself, from the grief of the ways the relationship was a fantasy, and from the process of extricating yourself. Life does get better. Knowing that you have consciously made decisions and taken actions on your own behalf will prove to be both therapeutic and empowering to you.

Sometimes when we talk about recovery, people think about returning to the state they were in prior to a difficult experience. In the instance of a toxic relationship, you may hope to return to "who you were" before meeting and getting involved with your narcissistic, borderline, or anti-social Ex. I would like gently to encourage you to shift your thinking away from returning to "who you were before" and toward accepting, exploring, and growing as who you are now and will be moving forward. I've never met or worked with anyone who wasn't changed by their experience of an intimate relationship with a toxic person. As I have already said, we can use the difficult experiences of these relationships as fertile ground for growth. You will never be the person you were before you got involved with your toxic Ex; that wouldn't benefit you anyway, given that it would leave you open to exploitation by someone similar in the future. As you move forward, understand that your recovery is recovery from the challenges of your toxic relationship, but not a return to who and how you were before. Your recovery, like that of many who have survived and exited toxic relationships, will ultimately allow you to "grow stronger in the broken places," approach the remainder of your life with greater wisdom and new skills, and hold yourself to a new standard for participating in relationships.

I've had the inspiration of bearing witness to many people reclaiming their lives from the grip of crazy-making relationships. The work is difficult and challenging, and things often get worse before they get better — always a sign that the relationship was toxic all along. Ultimately, survivors of toxic relationships do re-invent themselves and their lives in ways that reflect deeper authenticity and integrity, generate greater joy, and embrace greater measures of both freedom and connection. I wish all of this for you as you continue to use the skills of *The Five-Step Exit*. The world beyond the exit sign is vast and beautiful, indeed – and it, too, has suffered exploitation by narcissists and psychopaths centered on their own gain. We need you and your whole, miraculous, unique self here, able to show up, stay present, and make the world a better place.

RESOURCES

- Anderson, Donna. 2012. *Red Flags of Love Fraud* – 10 Signs You Are Dating a Sociopath. Trenton: Anderly Publishing.
- Ault, Amber, 2014. *The Wise Lesbian Guide to Getting Free From Crazy-Making Relationships and Getting On With Your Life*. Madison: Next Generation Books.
- Eden, Donna & Feinstein, David. 2008. *Energy Medicine: Balancing Your Body's Energies For Opimal Health, Joy, and Vitality*. New York: Tarcher. Eden, Donna & Feinstein, David. 2008.
- Gottman, John & Silver, Lynn. 2013. *What Makes Love Last? How to Build Trust and Avoid Betrayal*. New York: Simon & Schuster.
- Hare, Robert D. 1999. *Without Conscience*. New York: The Guilford Press.
- Kreisman, Jerold. 2010. *I Hate You — Don't Leave Me: Understanding Borderline Personality*. New York: Penguin.
- Mackenzie, Jackson. 2015. *Psychopath Free. Recovering from Emotionally Abusive Relationships with Narcissists. Sociopaths, & Other Toxic People*. New York: Berkley.
- Mason, Paul & Kreger, Randi. 2010. *Stop Walking On Eggshells: Taking Your Life Back When Someone You Care About Has Borderline Personality Disorder*. Oakland: New Harbinger Publications.

- Nhat Hanh, Thich. 2014. *No Mud, No Lotus*. Berkeley: Parallax Press.
- Renzetti, Claire. 1992. *Violent Betrayal: Partner Abuse in Lesbian Relationships*. Newbury Park, CA: Sage Publications.
- Salzburg, Sharon. 2011. *Loving-kindness: the Radical Art of Happiness*. Boston: Shambala Publications.
- Thomas, M.E., 2013. *Confessions of a Sociopath: A Life Spent Hiding in Plain Sight*. New York: Crown.
- Walker, Lenore E. 1979. *The Battered Woman*. New York: Harper and Row.
-

Hotlines

- National Domestic Violence Hotline: 1-800-799-SAFE (7233).
- National Suicide Prevention Lifeline: 1 (800) 273-8255
- The Trevor Project Suicide Prevention Support for LGBTQ Young People:
- 1-866-488-7386

ACKNOWLEDGMENTS

As we create happy, sane, inspiring relationships, we create spaces from which we can offer more love to a world desperately in need. My coaching and teaching centers on helping people know their true worth and that of others; as we honor our own gifts and build peaceful, securely attached relationships, we have more to bring to the project of improving the situation we all share here on Earth.

The model and practices presented in *The Five Step Exit* have evolved over the course of several years of clinical work with people in toxic partnerships. I am deeply grateful to the individuals, couples, and families who have entrusted me with their care. I find coaching both heterosexual and queer people and bearing witness as they transform their lives rewarding, inspiring, and sacred.

I offer continuing gratitude to the women who granted me interviews for a previous book, *The Wise Lesbian Guide to Getting Free From Crazy-making Relationships and Getting On With Your Life*. *The Five Step Exit* and my ongoing coaching and clinical work benefit from the generosity of those who agreed to share their histories of recovering from difficult relationships for the purpose of helping others.

My clinical thinking and practice owe their shape to the many teachers and colleagues to whom I would like to express my gratitude, including Dr. James McGloin, David LaCount, LCSW, the clinical staff of the Crisis Unit of Journey Mental Health, in Madison, Wisconsin, and the most excellent psychiatrists, social workers, and medical professionals with whom I regularly consult in the ER at St Mary's Hospital. I hope Rosanne Derdula, LCSW, knows by now how much I appreciate her, but because nobody can be reminded of that enough, I say it again here. I remain grateful to Sue Green and the women of OSU's Rape Education Prevention Program for their powerful impact on the skills I bring to the work I do.

Writing doula and medicine woman Julie Tallard Johnson set me on the path of letting go of academic writing, at least for a while, and two books have so far been delivered into the world as a result. Julie's mid-term consult on this text helped me carry it to delivery. The book also benefitted from a marvelous week-long workshop at the Key West Literary Seminar Writer's Workshop. There, I received the gracious, generous feedback and encouragement of a pod of 12 story tellers and fiction writers facilitated by novelist Manette Ansay, whose keen ear and kind encouragement kept us moving forward. To all of them, I am grateful.

Writing can be a lonely process, but it is made less so by the support of friends. For their encouragement, indulgence, and ongoing sharing of the journey in many different ways, I offer love and appreciation to Carla Corroto, Elizabeth McKenna, Nora Jacobson, Meghan Walsh & Mark Huth, Rebecca Kemble & Adam Chern, Ruth Goldman, Vicki Sussman, Pat Rodriguez, Kathrina Zippel, and Anne Tottero. Special thanks to Colleen Capper for our mutually beneficial writing accountability practice and to Helen Hazelmare, with whom I shared convivial co-writing sessions and general philosophizing in the summer of 2015. A lovely set of circumstances introduced me to the richly integrated Buddhist eco-feminist essays of Greta Gaard as I entered the final stage of completing this manuscript. Both the clarity and the poetry of her work inspired me; for that, and for an e-mail exchange that included mutual writerly encouragement, I offer a bow of gratitude.

Heather Ault proved a perfect choice for providing technical assistance in the material production of the book as it neared completion. We haven't figured out who our common ancestors might be yet, but I hope we do; until then, I'm grateful to have Heather as a member of my creative family system.

Of course, sometimes not writing and not talking about writing helps writers; I thank Mollie Ulm for being game for late-night stargazing and swim breaks and Leanne Cordisco for always being present when she is present – a gift even better than the food she creates, which is saying something.

The Five Step Exit evolved as I began to study tango; the Americanized variation of the dance focuses on a five step pattern with a slow/slow/quick/quick/slow rhythm that mirrors the pace of the stages in *The Five Step Exit*. The Argentine tango centers on improvisation after acquiring strong grounding in the basic steps, and offers opportunities to practice the skills of healthy, delightful, close relationships. I am grateful to my dance teachers, especially Joe Yang, Antonio Testolin, Steve Nasshan, Carla Coffey, and Christa Lessner, as well as to the students who have practiced with me over the last couple of years, for the ways dancing restores my creative energy and enhances my understanding of relationship dynamics. Abrazos!

Finally: at the heart of my writing, my desire to write, and my hope to make a difference in the world lives my gratitude to my mother, MaryLou Ault, whose example of a lifetime practice of kindness is always the standard to which I aspire.

ABOUT THE AUTHOR

A clinical sociologist, teacher, and writer, Amber Ault, Ph.D., MSW provides trainings to therapists and other professionals on supporting partners of personality-disordered people, working with clients at high risk of suicide, and on cultural competence with LGBTQ populations. She offers personal coaching to individuals and families locally in Madison, Wisconsin, as well as globally, thanks to the wonders of our increasing interconnectivity.

Made in the USA
Columbia, SC
25 October 2018